T0286805

Cambridge Elements ≡

Elements in Global Development Studies
edited by
Peter Ho
Zhejiang University
Servaas Storm
Delft University of Technology

INVESTOR STATES

Global Health at The End of Aid

Benjamin M. Hunter
University of Sussex

Shaftesbury Road, Cambridge CB2 8EA, United Kingdom

One Liberty Plaza, 20th Floor, New York, NY 10006, USA

477 Williamstown Road, Port Melbourne, VIC 3207, Australia

314–321, 3rd Floor, Plot 3, Splendor Forum, Jasola District Centre,
New Delhi – 110025, India

103 Penang Road, #05–06/07, Visioncrest Commercial, Singapore 238467

Cambridge University Press is part of Cambridge University Press & Assessment,
a department of the University of Cambridge.

We share the University's mission to contribute to society through the pursuit of
education, learning and research at the highest international levels of excellence.

www.cambridge.org
Information on this title: www.cambridge.org/9781009209557

DOI: 10.1017/9781009209564

First published 2023

A catalogue record for this publication is available from the British Library.

ISBN 978-1-009-20955-7 Paperback
ISSN 2634-0313 (online)
ISSN 2634-0305 (print)

Investor States

Global Health at The End of Aid

Elements in Global Development Studies

DOI: 10.1017/9781009209564
First published online: June 2023

Benjamin M. Hunter
University of Sussex
Author for correspondence: Benjamin M. Hunter,
benjamin.hunter@sussex.ac.uk

Abstract: This Cambridge Elements on Global Development Studies volume applies the lens of 'investor state' to a pattern of cross-border activities emerging at the end of aid. Using a series of case studies, the volume examines the growth of a trend where states operate as, with and for investors in the healthcare provision sectors of other nations. It sheds light on an evolving institutional landscape for global health in which state-owned development finance institutions, national development banks and sovereign wealth funds are becoming key financial stakeholders in healthcare systems. The trend has been gathering pace in the past 10–15 years in contexts of growing diversity for development financing and is driving the expansion of corporate-oriented models for healthcare provision that are liable to undermine already-strained progress towards achieving equitable access in healthcare globally.

This Element also has a video abstract: www.cambridge.org/hunter

Keywords: healthcare, financialisation, state capitalism, development cooperation, development finance

ISBNs: 9781009209557 (PB), 9781009209564 (OC)
ISSNs: 2634-0313 (online), 2634-0305 (print)

Contents

1 Introduction

The End of Aid

Official development assistance (ODA) flows to countries and territories on the DAC [Development Assistance Committee] List of ODA Recipients and to multi-lateral development institutions are: i. Provided by official agencies, including state and local governments, or by their executive agencies; and ii. Concessional (i.e. grants and soft loans) and administered with the promotion of the economic development and welfare of developing countries as the main objective. (OECD, 2022c)

The summary definition of development aid (or, in formal terms, official development assistance – ODA), established by the OECD Development Assistance Committee based on development objectives and concessional financing, may be familiar to many readers. Aspects of the contemporary history of aid are also often widely known: large-scale aid programmes emerged in the aftermath of World War Two as a tool for pursuing political and economic interests. The United States of America's (USA) aid-based strategy against communism in Europe – the Marshall Plan – set a precedent, and other governments from the geopolitical 'West' were drawn into the provision of aid in the 1950s and 1960s, partly because of US pressure and partly as an attempt to bolster their own international standing and trade. For former imperial powers such as the United Kingdom (UK), France and the Netherlands, aid offered a chance to maintain some semblance of influence and authority in the face of independence movements, vocal opposition to past imperialism and the dissolution of their empires. Governments in West Germany saw aid as an opportunity to bolster trade and boost German exports as they transitioned out of reparations payments (Schmidt, 2003), while Australia, New Zealand and Canada promoted social and economic development in the countries of the newly formed Commonwealth to promote trading within this group of states and buttress against the perceived threat of communism (Davis, 2011; D. Morrison, 1998). From an early stage the Japanese government, which by 1989 had become the world's largest contributor of development aid in absolute terms (USD 9.0 billion as compared to USD 7.7 billion committed by the USA – Katada, 2002), used aid for explicitly economic purposes such as boosting exports and securing flows of raw materials, combining it with various forms of non-concessional and private financing (Yasutomo, 1989).

Some of those political and economic motivations faded from view in the late twentieth century as the OECD's community of 'donors' converged around a set of shared moralities that recast state motivations for development financing along philanthropic lines. Though some governments have long prized ideas around poverty and sustainability in their development financing, for example those in Scandinavia (Selbervik & Nygaard, 2006), such ideas have tended to ebb and flow with other concerns depending on the domestic and geopolitical climate (van Dam & van Dis, 2014). By the turn of the century, development aid policies appealed to domestic audiences in liberal democracies who had grown to support aid quite widely, while at the same time signifying national leaders' global status and liberal values (Clarke, 2018; Honeyman, 2019). The sector was galvanised by visions of progress and hope, as economic growth and attainment of basic human needs in the Global South were not only desirable but realisable. States were 'graduating' from aid-recipient status to become aid senders in their own right, including 'Asian tiger' economies Singapore, Taiwan and South Korea, and many of the oil-exporting nations in the Middle East (OECD, 2022b). Development aid was endorsed as a way for the world's wealthiest states to fulfil moral obligations emanating from the 'Earth Summit' sustainability agenda and from the Millennium Development Goals.

But that narrative soon frayed. A wave of 'South-South Cooperation' was taking shape in which states varyingly referred to as 'rising powers' and 'emerging economies', and amongst which China is prominent, offered their own financing to other countries in the Global South. With varying degrees of concessionality, and often not reported to the OECD as ODA, these forms of development financing have faced accusations from Western counterparts that they prioritise nationalist economic and political agenda over development concerns (see special issue by Gray & Gills, 2016, for a range of perspectives on this). At the same time, the Global Financial Crisis shifted the domestic political landscape in many OECD countries, placing pressure on governments to justify aid budgets to an electorate at a time of cuts to other areas of public spending. There were significant incentives to use aid to pursue political and economic agendas, resulting in a phase of renewed economic nationalism in which aid is presented as a tool for 'national interests' and 'mutual benefits' (Gulrajani, 2017; Keijzer & Lundsgaarde, 2018; Mawdsley, 2017), and aid programmes focus on increasing demand for domestic goods and services (Mawdsley et al., 2018), and smoothing the path for companies to enter new foreign projects and markets (S. Brown, 2016). Humanitarianism and claims of philanthropy persist, but states also look to route their development financing through a range of instruments and institutions that operate on more commercial-like terms, 'beyond aid' (Janus et al., 2015).

For some time, commentators have predicted the 'end of aid' (Gill, 2018; Riddell, 1999), and we are now at a point where that end is increasingly tangible, even if it has not (yet) been fully realised. There are a growing number of states who have largely 'graduated' from aid-recipient status and who seek (and offer) new forms of financing to fuel economic development. At the same time, OECD states are moving away from an idea of aid that is narrowly defined instrument and has ostensibly philanthropic purposes, and towards a wider range of development financing instruments and motivations (Mawdsley & Taggart, 2022). The end of aid may be partial and incomplete, but in many contexts it has arrived. The aim of this Elements volume is to begin drawing attention to these changes and their implications as they play out in the arena of global health and its financing.[1]

The Study of Global Health and Its Financing

The biggest debates that have unfolded in academic literature on global health financing tend to be limited to the measurement of effects in one form or another: Has aid in the health sector led to improvements in health? And has it displaced funding from other sources such as those of governments in recipient countries? Development agencies make bold claims about 'lives saved' due to their funding, but in the scholarly literature the answers to these kinds of questions are more often contested, complex and contingent (see for example Coyne & Williamson, 2014; Feeny & Ouattara, 2013; Herzer, 2019). Much attention has been devoted to examining the effects of specific interventions so that these can be prioritised as targets for funding, in other words 'getting on with what works' (O. Campbell & Graham, 2006), yet this concern with producing evidence of effect becomes deeply problematic when it overlooks other systemic and social effects, and fails to consider the actors and interests whose interests are most advanced by these interventions (for examples of broader and more illuminating approaches, see Keshavjee, 2014; Pfeiffer, 2013). Health vouchers, on which I conducted research in the early-mid-2010s, are a powerful illustration. These were in vogue in parts of the global health community from the mid-2000s to mid-2010s, and organisations such as the US Agency for International Development and the Bill and Melinda Gates Foundation devoted significant resources to trialling and evaluating them in a range of settings. Systematic reviews that I and others performed on the resulting glut of evidence found positive *short-term* effects on uptake of some healthcare services, but also noted that the narrow design of evaluations meant *long-term* effects on healthcare usage, healthcare systems, and

---

[1] 'Global health' is a contested term with wide-ranging definitions that have been the subject of detailed examination elsewhere (see for example recent contributions by Hoffman & Cole, 2018; King & Koski, 2020; Salm et al., 2021). In writing the Element, I follow Lakoff (2010) and others in studying 'global health' not as a technocratic and politically neutral field of practice for improving health across borders, but rather as a global terrain of actors pursuing various interests through engagements with health-related projects and programming.

indeed health, were unknown (Hunter et al., 2017). Little attention had been paid
to the exclusion, marginalisation and gendered relations that were built into some
programmes by design (Gideon et al., 2017), and the market-based models for
welfare provision which incentivised exploitation of low-income users and programme workers (Hunter et al., 2020).

Instead, it is social science scholars whose work has offered more revealing
insights into global health financing and its evolution. 'Global health governance' scholarship, and related studies on the interactions of organisations in
international and other fora, have shed critical light on the influence of actors
such as states, civil society and corporate interest groups and their ability to
promote particular interventions or models for health (Cooper et al., 2007;
Harman, 2012; Kay & Williams, 2009; Maclean et al., 2009; McInnes et al.,
2014). Commentary in this area has tended to focus on the relative ascent/
decline in influence for specific organisations and their global health activities:
for example the World Bank (Baru & Jessani, 2000; Harman, 2009; Rao, 1999;
Sridhar et al., 2017; Youde, 2012), Gates Foundation (Harman, 2016; Mahajan,
2018; McGoey, 2015; Rushton & Williams, 2011; Youde, 2013) and World
Health Organization (T. M. Brown et al., 2006). This has taken place within
a broader context of neoliberal capitalism (Schrecker, 2020; Sell & Williams,
2020) where dominant actors in global health governance are able to promote
their preferred models for health and development within the global health
community; vouchers are one example, but others include infrastructure public-
private partnerships (Bayliss & Van Waeyenberge, 2017), performance-based
financing (Gautier et al., 2019), abstinence from sexual intercourse (Santelli
et al., 2017), and a host of technological solutions (McCoy & McGoey, 2011).
Geopolitical shifts are reflected in growing attendance to the activities performed by governments in countries varyingly grouped and labelled as 'Global
South' (Bartsch, 2009), 'Asian' (Tan et al., 2012), and 'BRICS' – Brazil,
Russia, India, China and South Africa (Gomez, 2009; Harmer & Buse, 2014;
Huang, 2020; Lisk & Šehović, 2020), with the Chinese government's activities
attracting particular attention (Chan et al., 2009; Cheng & Cheng, 2019; Grépin
et al., 2014; Husain & Bloom, 2020; Wang & Sun, 2014; Youde, 2018a, 2018b).
This body of literature reveals the interplay of multilateralism, philanthrocapit-
alism and geopolitics within wider networks of global health governance, but
has so far focused heavily on aid relations, offering limited insight into the end
of aid and its implications for global health.

This Elements volume addresses one activity emerging at the end of aid: how
a set of states from Europe and Asia are using their state-owned financing
institutions to invest in the healthcare systems of other countries. What is the
background to these activities and how have they grown and evolved? What is

the stated rationale for investment, what forms does investment take and which institutions are involved? Where are these investments being directed and what are the implications for healthcare provision and for global health? In addressing these questions, I argue that this phenomenon is gathering pace at the end of aid, bringing new sets of financial services and actors into global health, and driving specific models for healthcare provision that undermine already strained progress towards equitable access in healthcare. I show how public and private actors come together to expand healthcare provision models with little, if any, attention to issues of health equity; where they are discussed, they appear to be at best secondary concerns compared to business expansion and financial returns. In this the Element contributes to a small, but growing, body of literature on 'beyond aid' activities amongst OECD states (Doherty, 2011; Hamer & Kapilashrami, 2020; Hunter & Marriott, 2018; Hunter & Murray, 2015; Wemos, 2020), and on global health engagements by Asian states (Huang, 2020; Lisk & Šehović, 2020; Tan et al., 2012).

Structure of the Element

In the next two sections I set out the conceptual basis for the analysis. Section 2 uses key academic literature from the political economy study of development to show how recent trends for cross-border investments by states have been understood in terms of changes in aid policy and of the advent of 'new' state capitalisms. I use that as a springboard to set out a cross-cutting perspective that studies investor states: the institutions, activities and justifications through which states engage *as*, *with* and *for* investors in other countries. Section 3 reviews recent trends in the financing of global health and the accompanying shifts in its governance, and then outlines what has been documented so far in global health literature regarding the role of state investments.

Sections 4–7 present the empirical material in the form of a series of country cases. They show the growth trajectories of state investments and the state-owned financing institutions and private healthcare projects involved: the development finance institutions (DFI) of France and the UK (Section 4) and Sweden and the Netherlands (Section 5), national development banks of South Korea and Japan (Section 6), and sovereign wealth funds of Singapore and Malaysia (Section 7). These are financing institutions that invest in companies and projects using various mechanisms such as loans or purchases of equity; they tend not to work through the kinds of grants and concessional loans that are more commonly associated with the aid agencies of OECD states. The cases have been selected as illustrative of current trends and reflect a range of mechanisms to productively deploy national wealth, ranging from making returnable investments, to supporting national champion companies to expand overseas. The case studies build on a decade of my work studying development financing in healthcare. In each section the analysis is based on desk research conducted during July 2021–August 2022 and which involved detailed examination of policy documents, organisational reports and business press media coverage. The former provided official narratives, details of projects and investments and shifts in strategy; the latter complemented this with details on key events and announcements, 'puff piece' interviews revealing more implicit motivations and considerations, and less flattering information about disputes and losses that might be omitted from official publications. I collated these materials through examination of the websites of relevant organisations, supported by online searching in the Google search engine, using the names of projects and investors.

Common threads are then brought together in Section 8 with a summary of the cases and discussion of comparisons between them. The section then reflects on the nature of this emerging financialised regime for global health, the models of healthcare provision being expanded and areas for future research.

2 States and Development across Borders

The Elements volume draws inspiration from scholarship spanning two bodies of literature on the political economy of development and the cross-border activities of states: one primarily examines recent trends in development aid and its use by (typically OECD) donor states; the other examines the ways in which (typically non-OECD) states have engaged with the global economy. I briefly review key ideas from each of these literatures below, before setting out the cross-cutting concept of 'investor state' that informs the analysis of empirical materials in later sections.

Development Aid, Pluralism and Financialisation

The recent history of development aid is marked by key interrelated trends of growth, privatisation and financialisation. After a trend of decreases in annual aid commitments amongst OECD member states during the 1990s following the end of the Cold War, the 2000s saw a reversal in which total aid commitments nearly doubled between 2000 and 2015; jumping from USD 77 billion in 2000 to USD 129 billion by 2010 and USD 140 billion by 2015 (OECD, 2022c). The trend was driven by the aspirations of the Millennium Development Goals, and the development component of the United States of America's (USA) War on Terror (Mohan & Mawdsley, 2007), and has been dominated by the largest OECD economies of USA, Germany, UK, Japan and France, which contributed a combined USD 113 billion in development aid in 2020 (OECD, 2021).

With that growth in aid, however, came concerns with coordination and accountability, as well as heightened awareness that aid was increasing at a slower rate than other forms of financing and was likely to reach a ceiling level.[2] The traditional donor-driven model for aid programming came under increased scrutiny and a series of policy discussions and events took place during the 2000s, framed around the issue of better designing and delivering aid in pursuit of 'aid effectiveness'. By the early 2010s, and the Fourth High Level Forum on Aid Effectiveness in Busan (2011), development *aid* was being repositioned as development *cooperation*, placing greater emphasis on partnership and mutuality (Silva et al., 2021). This move also appealed to the non-OECD states whose own development financing did not necessarily conform to OECD standards for reporting ODA but was being seen as part of a movement for 'South-South cooperation' that could avoid the kinds of neo-colonial donor-recipient power asymmetries that have undermined the West's development aid paradigm (Quadir, 2013).

The Busan conference on aid effectiveness was also notable in its embrace for private sector participation in development financing. Such participation is not new, as aid programmes over the past forty years have been designed and implemented by private consultancies, with the USA and its 'development-industrial complex' leading the charge (Roberts, 2014). Private industry has been positioned as a valid target for development aid, with development organisations loosely dividing activities into private sector *development* (building up private enterprise as a pathway to economic development, job creation and wealth) and private sector *engagement* (encouraging leading national and international businesses to incorporate ideas around human development into their strategies and practices). Initiatives like the United Nations Global Compact encouraged participation by multinational corporations in global policy processes, and by the time of the Busan High Level Forum on Aid Effectiveness, they had become embedded within this sector (Mah, 2018; Mawdsley et al., 2014).

A range of forms of privatisation in development have been bundled together through the language of 'public-private partnership' that took hold in the early 2000s. Partnership was a notion enshrined by Millennium Development Goal 8 (to develop a global partnership for development) and could be applied as an umbrella term for public-private arrangements ranging from corporate social responsibility programmes to global fora such as the UN's Global Compact (Buse & Harmer, 2004; Languille, 2017). The term also provided cover for

---

[2] The growth of alternative resource flows such as remittances and foreign direct investment has outpaced development aid and accounts for the vast majority of funds received by low- and middle-income countries (Silva et al., 2021).

public-private arrangements that might be more controversial, such as the widening involvement of for-profit organisations in social sectors like health-care and education (Gideon & Unterhalter, 2017). It is a term that not only masks the underlying transfers in resources taking place, and the newfound policy influence private organisations can gain, but does so using neutralist terminology (of partnership, cooperation and engagement) that is 'appealing and seductive' (Verger, 2012).

The third trend, and perhaps most pertinent to note here, is that of financia-lisation. The social science concept of financialisation refers to the 'increasing role of financial motives, financial markets, financial actors and financial institutions in the operation of the domestic and international economies' (Epstein, 2005, p. 3). The concept's use in the study of global development has been valuable in highlighting the growing range of sectors, actors and phenomena that are subject to, and distorted by, the logics of finance (Mader et al., 2020; Storm, 2018). It is a process that sees life and society transformed in ways that individualise and collateralise, creating new zones for investment and producing saleable assets that can be traded by financial actors and in financial markets.

With regard to development financing, a financialisation lens draws attention to the growing role of private financial capital within the development practi-tioner community, and the latter's reorientation to attract, deliver and recom-pense said private capital (Mawdsley, 2016). Momentum has been growing since at least the Global Financial Crisis to embed the practices and agents of financial services industries into development financing systems, and these ideas began to appear in outcome documents from influential global confer-ences such as the second International Conference on Financing for Development in Doha (2008) and the Busan High Level Forum on Aid Effectiveness. The idea that aid could be used to 'leverage' or 'catalyse' private investment began to attract the interest of a financial services industry that saw the commercial value of positioning as socially oriented investors focusing on 'emerging markets'; one of the most prominent was Dubai-based Abraaj Capital, whose Chief Executive Officer Arif Naqvi championed the idea of 'partnership capital' – public and multilateral loan guarantees and risk mitiga-tion that would subsidise participation by private investment companies (Naqvi, 2016).[3] But it was at the Third International Conference on Financing for Development in Addis Ababa (2015), timed to run alongside the Sustainable

---

[3] Abraaj Chief Executive Officer Arif Naqvi was a darling of the development financing world in the early-mid-2010s, receiving plaudits for working in emerging markets and appearing at World Economic Forum events in Davos, and he reportedly kept a picture of him with Bill Gates on his office desk (S. Clark & Louch, 2021 p. 172). But accusations of fraud in 2019 resulted in

Development Goal (SDG) discussions, where the idea really gained traction (United Nations, 2015). The notion of a sustainable development 'financing gap' – an estimated USD 2.5 trillion annual shortfall in financing needed to achieve the SDGs – was becoming increasingly accepted amongst much of the development community, along with the assumption that aid flows would never be sufficient to fill this gap (see the *Billions to Trillions* report published in the run-up to the conference by World Bank and International Monetary Fund, 2015). Pressure was building to pursue alternative resources such as domestic resource mobilisation (primarily in the form of taxation) and private finance, with the latter becoming more prominent since.

The narrative now championed by multilateral and private financial actors is of a 'financing gap', a private finance solution and the need for states to reorient towards attracting and subsidising that private finance. It has met a receptive audience amongst OECD states where an economic nationalism engendered by the Global Financial Crisis had already seen development aid reframed along overtly self-interested lines. National DFIs – institutions that historically used equity investments, loans, loan guarantees, risk insurance and sometimes grants to support manufacturing companies in low- and middle-income countries on the premise of economic growth and job creation and which existed largely on the fringes of mainstream development financing (Savoy et al., 2016) – were being handed larger budgets and expanded remits to cover new geographies and sectors (see Table 1 for a list of European DFIs by size). OECD states, as part of a 'modernisation' process for development cooperation, began to press for new definitions and indicators that could incorporate a wider range of development financing beyond ODA. A set of reporting arrangements were agreed for 'private sector instruments' (primarily loans and equity investments made by DFIs), while progress has been made to formalise a new indicator – 'total official support for sustainable development' (TOSSD) – that will capture a wider range of development financing commitments than just ODA. States can even report private finance as part of TOSSD as long as 'a causal link between the provision of the private finance and the official intervention can be documented' (OECD, 2022d, p. 15). Wrapped in language of partnership and mutuality, these moves have sought to legitimise a pivot towards financial interests and practices, and towards the kind of self-interested provision of development financing that aroused concern when associated with non-OECD states.

The current scenario has been described by Gabor (2021) as reflecting a 'Wall Street Consensus' paradigm in which states function to 'de-risk' private

a spectacular fall from grace that saw Abraaj collapse and Naqvi facing fraud charges and 291 years of imprisonment in the USA.

Table 1 List of European DFIs by investment portfolio value

Country	Development Financing Institution	Portfolio value, as of end−2021 (EUR millions)
UK	British International Investment (BII) (formerly Commonwealth Development Corporation and CDC Group)	9,993
Germany	Deutsche Investitions und Entwicklungsgesellschaft (DEG)	9,242
France	Proparco (formerly Société de Promotion et de Participation pour la Coopération Economique)	8,740
Netherlands	Financierings-Maatschappij voor Ontwikkelingslanden (FMO)	8,448
Norway	Norfund	2,695
Spain	Compañía Española de Financiación del Desarrollo (COFIDES)	1,884
Austria	Oesterreichische Entwicklungsbank (OeEB)	1,466
Finland	Finnfund	1,140
Denmark	Investeringsfonden for Udviklingslande (IFU)	1,134
Belgium	Belgian Investment Company for Developing countries (BIO)	807
Switzerland	Swiss Investment Fund for Emerging Markets (SIFEM)	796
Sweden	Swedfund	696
Italy	Cassa Depositi e Prestiti (CDP) and Società italiana per le imprese all'estero (SIMEST)	626 and 338
Portugal	Sociedade para o Financiamento do Desenvolvimento (SOFID)	12

Source: Association of European Development Finance Institutions (2022)

investments. In a global policy context where attracting private finance is increasingly seen as paramount for development, the role of the state has become one of engineering policy and infrastructure to produce the asset classes into which global finance can invest. Gabor's analysis focused on the states in which the infrastructure projects take place (i.e. financing recipients), and the multilateral organisations advocating de-risking, but other states play a role too, as advocates and (co-)investors in their own right. Mawdsley and Taggart (2022) note the role of DFIs as investors in processes of de-risking, situating the growing stature of these financing institutions within a wider offer of development financing options (aid and non-aid) by OECD states; it is seen as a way for these OECD states to 'better compete with Southern actors – and each other' (p. 9).

Developmentalism and 'New' State Capitalisms

Running largely in parallel to the above is analysis around the expanding role of the state in global economic activity. One prominent and long-standing concept in this area is that of the 'developmental state' – a term coined by political economists seeking to understand and explain the economic development models pursued by countries in East Asia in the mid-twentieth century. Chalmers Johnson (1982) first used the term in reference to the era's 'Japanese miracle': a period of rapid industrialisation and technological specialisation based on a dominant civil service bureaucracy and government industrial policy-making. Juxtaposed with the USA's 'regulatory state' (where public policy centred on protecting market processes) and Communist planned economy models (that centred on public ownership), Johnson argued that Japan's developmental state reflected a nationalist economic model with public subsidies, infrastructure, and other support for Japanese companies in priority industries; protection for these companies from international competitors, and government oversight determining 'what industries ought to exist and what industries are no longer needed' (p. 19). The concept of the developmental state caught on as other commentators found value in applying the term to other countries and territories in the region, including South Korea, Taiwan, China, Singapore and Hong Kong (Douglass, 1994; White & Wade, 1984), and subsequently a wider range of states. It has been understood not as a readily defined and prescriptive model for economic development, but rather as a set of time-specific characteristics, processes and trajectories that could be discerned through retrospective analysis, and which emphasised state coordination of export-led economic growth (Caldentey, 2008; Wade, 2018; Wong, 2004; Woo-Cumings, 1999).

The interventions of the developmental state in economic activity in the mid-late twentieth century provide the backdrop for a more recent set of trends that sees states engaging more extensively and as owners of capital in domestic and overseas settings. State-owned entities, particularly from some Asian settings (China is prominent but not alone), are growing in value and reach, becoming increasingly transnational in their operations. This has been understood as a departure from the more domestically focused developmental state and instead represents a new phase of 'state capitalism'; a concept that has been applied to range of phenomena in the study of state-capital relations over a relatively long history (see Sperber, 2019, for an account of its historical use, ambiguities and contestations). Recent journal special issues and other work by Alami and colleagues have done much to elaborate a contemporary period of 'new' state capitalism (Alami, Dixon, Gonzalez-Vicente, et al., 2021; Alami et al., 2022; Alami & Dixon, 2020b, 2021) that sees significant 'expansion of the state's role as promoter, supervisor, regulator, and owner of capital' (Alami et al., 2022, p. 12). It is characterised by an expansion of different forms of state-owned capital and a wider statism that is not just 'proactive' (Wright et al., 2021) but 'strong' (Alami & Dixon, 2020a).

It is the transnationalisation of state capitalism that is of particular interest here. Commentators have highlighted a range of state-owned entities which operate transnationally, and which are increasingly recognised by leading multilateral institutions as prominent actors in development processes (Alami, Dixon, & Mawdsley, 2021). Two institutional forms are particularly pertinent to this Elements volume: national development banks and sovereign wealth funds. The former have been created as a mechanism to provide long-term financing (loans, loan guarantees, risk insurance, equity investments and grants) for industrial development (Musacchio et al., 2017), often in post-war and newly independent states in the mid-late twentieth century (Griffith-Jones & Ocampo, 2018). Though similar to Anglo-European DFIs in terms of their focus on sponsoring enterprise and economic growth, national development banks have historically tended to focus on domestic growth rather than growth in other countries. National development banks were an important component in the developmental state model of some Asian countries, as well as outside this region (see for example Hochstetler & Montero, 2013, on Brazil's Banco Nacional de Desenvolvimento Econômico e Social – BNDES). The rapid growth of lending by such banks in recent decades is used to facilitate the international expansion of domestic companies, including the large, well-connected corporations sometimes referred to as 'national champions' (Bremmer, 2009), and is a trend that has seen their lending surpass that of the multilateral development banks (Kring & Gallagher, 2019). National development banks often have total assets that far exceed those of DFIs, for example Japan Bank for International Cooperation and Korea Development Bank (Section 6) have USD 162 billion and USD 235 billion in assets, respectively, while China Development Bank has USD 2 trillion (Kring & Gallagher, 2019).

The second organisational form of interest here – sovereign wealth funds – were initially envisaged as a way to manage the wealth being accumulated by oil-exporting nations in the twentieth century (G. Clark et al., 2013). They aimed to use judicious investing of this wealth to secure its value in the longer-term, and other states soon followed suit as they sought to manage foreign currency reserves they were accumulating due to rapidly growing export indus-tries (Klitzing et al., 2010). One recent trend has been for these funds to function not as passive 'rainy day' savings accounts, but rather as active investors looking to generate more substantial returns for the fund's state owner. Accordingly, the managers of these funds have looked to diversify their port-folios through investments in a broader range of products, sectors and markets, while institutional reforms have been introduced in the hope of emulating the practices of private investment companies, though the imperatives of the state ownership remain (Dixon, 2022). Like national development banks, they are often much larger than DFIs in terms of total assets, with Khazanah, Temasek and Government of Singapore Investment Corporation (GIC) (Malaysia and Singapore, Section 7) having total assets of USD 30 billion, USD 497 billion, and USD 690 billion, respectively; the world's largest sovereign wealth fund – that of the Norwegian government – is valued at USD 1.3 trillion (Sovereign Wealth Fund Institute, 2022).

The transnationalisation of these kinds of institutions is not, however, without resistance. There are well-documented fears, often voiced from OECD settings, that foreign state ownership of strategic industries such as energy and commu-nications represents a threat to national sovereignty and security (Cuervo-Cazurra, 2018), as well as a wider set of concerns encompassing regulatory compliance, state subsidies that make state-owned entities difficult to compete with, and other forms of state interference in their running (Balbuena, 2016; Bremmer, 2009). The result is a somewhat uncomfortable relationship between the institutions of new state capitalism and the institutions that have long dominated global development. The former represent a potential source of financing that could help to plug the sustainable development financing gap, yet they also challenge decades-old apprehension amongst some OECD states and multinational organisations regarding public ownership and intervention in the economy. Multilateral and other leading development organisations have tried to balance these competing stances through a rather selective encourage-ment of national development banks and/or sovereign wealth funds to align themselves with the goals and projects of sustainable development (OECD, 2015; UNCTAD, 2014; World Bank, 2013a), but in such a way as to not endorse state ownership and to 'preserve and further enshrine the centrality of market regulation' (Alami, Dixon, & Mawdsley, 2021, p. 1313).

Investor States

In this Elements volume I attempt to bridge the two bodies of work outlined above using the lens of *investor state*. Scholarship on the political economy of development frequently adopts state-oriented lenses to conceptualise particular forms and changes in society, positioning the 'state' as a territorially bound authority with varying degrees of autonomy from private and other interests (Skocpol, 1985). State institutions such as its legislature, courts and government bureaucracies evolve over time, as do their ways of working, resulting in significant variation in state roles and functions across time and space, and a range of concepts have been adopted by social science scholars to draw attention to specific features and transformations in the state. For example, attempts by politicians and allied technocrats in the late twentieth century to 'roll-back' intervention by states in some spheres of life, in line with neoliberal political and economic doctrine of the time, led to the rapid growth in public contracting of private organisations and to state-forms conceptualised as 'hollow' (Milward & Provan, 2000), 'congested' (Skelcher, 2000), or just outright 'neoliberal' (Harvey, 2005).

'Investor state' here refers to the institutions, activities and justifications through which states engage *as*, *with* and *for* investors in other countries. In this it cuts across different groupings (OECD / non-OECD), institutions (DFIs / national development banks / sovereign wealth funds), and financing modalities (aid / non-aid), to enable a more comprehensive view of the current development landscape and the zones in which various state institutions are operating. It is not a new state-form, as the pooled resources of the state have long been invested in domestic and overseas projects, but what is new is the combined scope, apparatus and rhetorical infrastructure through which these activities are taking place, and here I draw particular attention to resources being transferred *transnationally* into the *private segments of social sectors* in other countries, using *state financing institutions*, and delivered and framed on the basis of *returns*.

The study of investor states in relation to healthcare provision combines analysis of the specific activities, locations and mechanisms for investment, with an understanding of the stated motivations, justifications and achievements for such work. It looks for patterning within and across the activities of different states, such as overlapping geographies and institutional mimicry, as well as distinguishing features and exceptions. It pays particular attention to the alliances of public and private organisations that come together to make (co-)investments, to build chains of corporate hospitals, and to champion the prospects for investment in future. It is a perspective that enables us to better understand how the global health landscape is being repopulated and remade at the end of aid.

3 Trends in Global Health Financing and Governance

For global health, the end of aid means moving away from a set of institutions
and activities that propelled health to the top of the development agenda during
the 2000s. In this section I show how global health actors and objectives made
substantial gains during much of the Millennium Development Goal era but
then plateaued after the Global Financial Crisis. In that context, various actors
have sought to expand the role of private finance in global health, marking an
extension of pre-existing trends to increase private sector involvement in global
health. This has created a policy landscape in which investor state roles in global
health have grown, with participation justified on the basis of the sustainable
development financing gap and the capital needs of corporate healthcare
providers.

The Global Health Financing Plateau

While ODA has been used as a measure of development aid in global development (see previous section), a slightly different gauge has been used by many
agencies to trace financing flows in global health: *development assistance for
health*. This has been conceived and monitored by the USA-based Institute for
Health Metrics and Evaluation (IHME),[4] and is defined as 'the financial and in-
kind contributions from major development agencies to low-income and middle-income countries for maintaining or improving population health' (Chang
et al., 2019, p. 2235). The concept of development assistance for health is
slightly broader than ODA as it includes additional sources of information
and commitments, and while it has some limitations in the extent to which it
captures development financing beyond ODA (Bendavid et al., 2017), it is
widely regarded as the most comprehensive assessment that exists for tracking
development financing in global health.

The IHME's analyses of development assistance for health show that these
flows nearly trebled in size in the space of a decade between 2000 and 2009,
from USD 13 billion to USD 32 billion; increasing at a rate of 11.3 per cent
annually between 2000 and 2009, compared to 5.7 per cent in the preceding
decade (Dieleman et al., 2016). That period has been referred to by some
commentators as a 'golden era' for the field of global health due to rapid
increases in the availability of financing and technologies to address health
needs (Kickbusch & Szabo, 2014; J. Morrison, 2012). The aspirational goals
and targets of the Millennium Development Goals, propelled child health

---

[4] IHME has relied heavily on funding from the Gates Foundation, including USD 105 million when
founded in 2007 and a further USD 279 million in 2017. Its production of global health metrics
has contributed to the sidelining of the World Health Organization's in this area (Mahajan, 2019).

(Goal 4), maternal health (Goal 5), and HIV, tuberculosis and other infectious diseases (Goal 6), to the forefront of development planning and programmes. Prominent politicians, academics and practitioners were advocating for increased support for countries beleaguered by the HIV pandemic and persisting concerns with maternal and newborn deaths, and inspired an outpouring of international financing to meet these health challenges. In absolute terms, most of the financing came from Anglo-European member states of the OECD: USA, UK, Germany, France, Netherlands, Sweden, Canada, Norway and Spain (Dieleman et al., 2016). Just two countries – the USA and UK – were responsible for approximately one-third of development assistance for health in that period. Japan was the largest sender outside of those countries, committing USD 920 million in development assistance for health in 2009 (Institute for Health Metrics and Evaluation, 2019).

The 'golden era' for global health even persisted through the immediate aftermath of the Global Financial Crisis. Tracking of development assistance for health shows that funding rose during 2007–2011, fuelled in part by increased commitments from some OECD countries such as the USA, Canada, Japan, Australia and Norway. Some actors from beyond the OECD had become important too. Private philanthropy had been steadily growing during the 2000s, led by the Gates Foundation, and between 2007 and 2011 annual commitments from private philanthropy nearly doubled, from USD 3.3 to 6.2 billion. Meanwhile non-OECD countries were substantially increasing their commitments: the Chinese government doubled its aid commitments in the health sector between 2007 and 2012, to surpass USD 600 million (Micah et al., 2019); while annual development assistance for health from governments in the Middle East and North Africa (particularly United Arab Emirates, Saudi Arabia and Kuwait) collectively reached USD 600 million in 2013, having trebled from 2007 levels (Zhao et al., 2020). Such commitments were still relatively small compared to commitments by, for example, the USA, but nonetheless revealing of growing plurality in global health financing.

The increases in total development assistance for health that took place in the immediate aftermath of the Global Financial Crisis masked underlying disruption to funding from specific OECD countries. Some of the largest contributors of development assistance for health, including the UK, France, the Netherlands and Spain, quickly froze and reduced their commitments. Drops in funding from the UK and France were short-lived and returned to previous levels within one or two years, but for Netherlands and Spain funding continued to fall over the subsequent decade. In the case of Spain, which experienced a sovereign debt crisis in the aftermath of the Global Financial Crisis, even by 2019 development assistance for

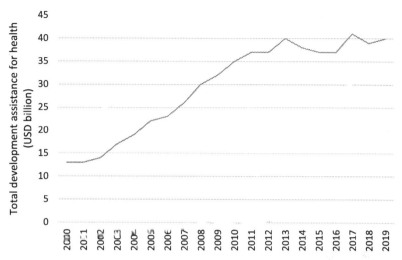

Figure 1 Total development assistance for health, 2000–2019

Source: Data from IHME (2020)

health was still just one-quarter of the USD 860 million committed in 2008 (IHME, 2022).

By the early 2010s, total development assistance for health began to plateau (Figure 1), as the longer-term political and economic repercussions of the Global Financial Crisis manifested in the form of austerity programmes for public spending. Many key contributors including the USA began cutting their global health spending, and between 2010 and 2015 development assistance for health rose at a rate of just 1.2 per cent annually, as opposed to 11.3 per cent annually in the preceding ten years, and those small increases were largely due to the continued growth in private philanthropy and other non-state spending (Dieleman et al., 2016). The Gates Foundation, for example, had become one of the largest funders of the World Health Organization, second only to the USA (van de Pas & van Schaik, 2014). The plateau continued into the second half of the decade, and by 2019 development assistance for health stood at USD 40 billion, just USD 5 billion more than in 2010.[5]

Financialisation in Global Health Governance

The global health financing plateau has been accompanied by several inter-related trends in global health governance that provided a policy context in which investor states could grow. First, there had been growing engagement

---

[5] It is only since the onset of the COVID-19 pandemic that development assistance for health has risen substantially again (IHME, 2022).

with private organisations in the *financing and governance* of global health since the 1990s. As noted above, private philanthropy had become a major feature in the financing of global health, with multinational corporations making large financial or in-kind donations, often through philanthropic foundations. Although the financial services industry was not prominent in those activities, the trend had normalised the incursion of private sources of funding into health programming. The creation of 'global health initiatives' at the turn of the century, in response to the needs of health-related Millennium Development Goals, formalised private involvement in global policy processes as board and council positions were given to representatives from multinational corporations, offering new avenues for influence (Buse & Harmer, 2004). It is only relatively recently that critiques of this deepening public-private engagement have become more mainstream in global health, coalescing around critiques of the 'commercial determinants of health' and the lobbying of associated industries (Kickbusch, 2012).

Second, the normalisation of involvement by private organisations in the *delivery* of health programmes and, of particular interest here, healthcare services. This has a longer history in which structural adjustment–era reforms encouraged by the World Bank and others during the 1980s and 1990s are prominent (Rao, 1999). It has passed increasingly unchallenged since the turn of the century as an apparently pragmatic response to the needs of healthcare systems (Mills, 2014), with interest revolving around policies that would organise private sectors within healthcare systems and an insurance-based vision for 'universal health coverage' (Birn et al., 2016; Kumar, 2019). Although some commentators have pointed to a diversity of provider types, ranging from small informal providers to large corporate hospital chains (Mackintosh et al., 2016), most research has focused on the former and not the latter. Yet it is the latter which are emerging most visibly in middle-income contexts and triggering far-reaching transformations across the healthcare system, segmenting access to healthcare. Most importantly here, the corporate entities which run private hospital chains offer a platform for entry by global financial capital into healthcare systems, through the debt and shareholding relationships which global investors can build with healthcare corporations (Hunter & Murray et al., 2019).

Third, the World Bank, Gates Foundation and other international organisations have been experimenting for fifteen years with mechanisms to bring private finance into global health. In 2006, global health initiative Gavi launched its International Finance Facility for Immunisation, an early forerunner of this trend, that sought to quickly raise financial capital from private markets by issuing what became known as 'vaccine bonds'. Investors purchase the bonds, providing immediate funds to Gavi, and are then repaid (with interest) over several years and decades from a USD 8 billion fund provided by governments primarily in OECD countries (UK, France, Italy, Norway, the Netherlands, Australia, Spain and Sweden), along with Brazil and South Africa. The World Bank's attempts to expand roles for private financial capital in healthcare are relatively well documented (see Hunter & Murray, 2019; Sridhar et al., 2017; Stein & Sridhar, 2018), but less is known about some of the other actors involved. The Gates Foundation, for example, worked with the World Bank (through its private investment arm the International Finance Corporation – IFC) and healthcare corporate Netcare on an initiative to promote investment in private healthcare systems in Africa (IFC, 2008b; see Marriott & Hamer, 2014 for a critical review of the initiative). Their *Business of Health in Africa* report, produced by McKinsey, included proposals to increase investment by combining development finance with private finance (an approach sometimes referred to as 'blended finance') and offering 'patient capital' that would support expansion without the need for immediate gains. S. Clark and Louch (2021) have reported the existence of a second McKinsey publication but that was never made publicly available and that advocated for creation of a private equity fund that could invest in healthcare companies in low- and middle-income countries. The Africa Health Fund was soon born, with initial investments from the IFC, Gates Foundation and Germany's DEG; the fund's subsequent acquisition by Naqvi's Abraaj in 2012 appears to have been important in legitimising Abraaj's involvement in global health and paving way for Abraaj's Growth Markets Health Fund.

Fourth, while many OECD countries afforded some protection to the *volume* of their global health financing after the Global Financial Crisis, the logics and justifications for development aid were becoming more explicitly driven by nationalist, often economic, concerns. As noted in Section 2, during the early 2010s some governments began to place more emphasis on framing their development programmes around notions of mutual benefit and promoting their own 'national interests'. In health national interests manifested with support for 'global health diplomacy' as an arena through which states could pursue 'soft power' relations and trade interests (Kickbusch & Kokeny, 2013). Security had also become a central concept within global health programming and scholarship (Rushton, 2011), populated by regimes of militarised and security-oriented actors and interests (Lakoff, 2017), and failures in the international response to the 2013–2016 Ebola epidemic in Western Africa only served to further this process of securitisation (Heymann et al., 2015). The growing attention being afforded to blended finance in global development fora, and in particular the idea that instruments like loans and equity investments could be used in a wider range of social sectors such as health, opened up new opportunities for governments interested in generating economic returns from their development aid budgets.

Fifth, the wider global development context, including discussions surrounding the Third International Conference on Financing for Development in Addis Ababa (2015) and the accompanying rise of the Wall Street Consensus, added impetus to efforts already underway to reorient multi- and bilateral organisations towards catalysing private finance. The agenda set out in the SDGs spanned a much broader range of public health issues than the Millennium Development Goals (Buse & Hawkes, 2015), and in doing so created additional needs for financing to achieve this enlarged agenda for global health. This need was then quantified when the USD 2.5 trillion 'financing gap' was disaggregated to produce an SDG3-specific calculation of USD 371 billion required annually (Stenberg et al., 2017). Given that development assistance for health was plateauing at approximately USD 37 billion annually, proponents of alternative financing mechanisms could point to a substantial financing gap as justification for new approaches involving public and private finance.

Investor States Rising

The result of these intersecting trends has been a steady increase in public and private investments in overseas healthcare systems, which I have tracked using organisation websites and press media coverage.[6] Multilateral DFIs have been prominent in this, with the IFC's direct commitments to private healthcare provision projects quadrupling from around USD 50 million annually in the run-up to the Global Financial Crisis, to USD 200 million during the decade afterwards. Unlike development assistance for health, the IFC's investments in healthcare did not increase markedly during much of global health's golden era, but rather picked up pace as the trends detailed in Section 2 began to converge. Regional development banks such as the African Development Bank and the European Bank for Reconstruction and Development have played important roles in specific regions and projects too (see later sections). Their investments are often made alongside contributions by other organisations such as philanthropic foundations, private equity firms and state-owned financing institutions. In this, the involvement of multilateral organisations offers a degree of political and financial de-risking, due to the standing of multilateral institutions and/or

---

[6] For more details and an indicative list of investments, see Hunter and Marriott (2018). The tracking only includes *direct* investments made by states in healthcare provision. Many financing institutions also make investments *indirectly* via intermediary private companies known as fund managers; however, details of the investments then made by those fund managers are not always shared in the public domain.

arrangements that involve private investors being prioritised for the return of capital should an investment project encounter problems.

Private fund management companies have also been important, functioning as a platform to pool investments from multiple organisations and then spread investment risk across a portfolio of companies. Large companies such as USA-based TPG, as well as smaller ones with a sectoral focus such as Singapore-based Quadria, now boast sizeable healthcare portfolios that blend the financing of multilateral, bilateral and private investors. In many cases there is a regional geographical focus for where investments are made, for example Africa (Table 2) or Asia (see discussion on UK use of fund managers in Section 4).

But of particular interest here are the investments being made by states. DFIs have tended to be the most transparent of the different types of state financing institutions in terms of releasing information on their investments. Between 2000 and 2017, national DFIs committed USD 1.5 billion to healthcare providers, of which 99 per cent came after 2007, and 90 per cent after 2013. Although these figures are likely to be underestimates, as they rely on public sources and do not include indirect investments made via fund managers, they nonetheless show a sharp increase in this area in the past ten years – the same period as global health's financing plateau. Nonetheless, they remain small in comparison to the USD 40 billion committed as development assistance for health by public and private organisations annually.

Amongst the DFIs investing directly in private healthcare provision up to 2017, the leading institution in terms of total investment size was the USA's Overseas Private Investment Corporation,[7] with France's Proparco, Germany's DEG, FinDev Canada and the UK's BII also making sizeable commitments. Two-thirds of the direct commitments, including almost all of those made by the USA and Canada, were loans provided to finance the construction of Turkey's integrated health campuses (see Section 6). If those projects are excluded from the analysis, then three DFIs, Proparco (51 per cent), DEG (22 per cent) and BII (21 per cent), together accounted for 94 per cent of total direct DFI investment in private healthcare projects.

The extent of involvement by other states and other financing institutions is harder to discern when investment portfolios are not routinely reported publicly as they are for some DFIs. But as I show later in this Element, healthcare investments are not restricted to Anglo-European states. South Korea and Japan (Section 6), and Singapore and Malaysia (Section 7), have invested significant sums in pursuit of their own interests in the healthcare sectors of other countries.

---

[7] In 2019, the USA's Overseas Private Investment Corporation was merged with the US export credit agency, the Development Credit Authority, to create a new DFI: the US International Development Finance Corporation.

Table 2 Early examples of Africa-focused health funds

Fund name and capitalisation	Fund manager	Investors
Africa Health Fund – USD 105 million	Aureos Capital	First closing attracted investments from: • Multilaterals – IFC and the African Development Bank • Bilateral – DEG • Philanthropic foundation – Gates Foundation Second closing attracted investments from: • Multilateral – Development Bank of Southern Africa • Bilateral – Norfund and Proparco • Philanthropic foundations – Elma Foundation, Maria Wrigley Trust • Other private investors – ASN Bank
Investment Fund for Health in Africa – USD 66 million	Africa Health Systems Management	• Multilaterals – IFC and African Development Bank • Bilateral – FMO • Philanthropic foundations – Stichting Social Investor Foundation for Africa (which itself combines grants from financial services companies Achmea and SNS-Reaal, life insurance company AEGON, alcohol company Heineken, oil company Shell, and Unilever) • Other private investors – Goldman Sachs, Pfizer, Dutch pension fund Algemene Pensioen Groep
Investment Fund for Health in Africa II – USD 137 million	Africa Health Systems Management	• Multilateral – IFC and European Investment Bank • Bilateral – FMO • Other private investors – Achmea

Indeed, many DFI investments are dwarfed by those made by national development banks and sovereign wealth funds. This Elements volume provides an initial exploration of activities performed by these states and their financing institutions, and the basis for their future study.

4 UK, France and Development Finance Institutions

A small number of OECD states have been prominent in the growth of investment in overseas private healthcare projects. In this section I trace the activities of two states whose DFIs have been at the vanguard of this movement: the UK and France. The section shows how DFIs from these countries have invested equity and loans in a wide range of overseas private healthcare providers, often in coordination with other bi- or multilateral DFIs, as they chase new post-aid positions in the global political economy. Social development justifications which were initially employed to justify such work have faded in contexts of economic nationalism. These states are becoming key stakeholders in the expansion of corporate models for private healthcare provision, facilitating the current and future penetration of the financial services industry into the healthcare sector.

UK

When the UK government created the Colonial Development Corporation in 1948, as an institution to invest in overseas companies and support growth, it was an early attempt to foster private sector activity on a financially returnable basis and within a development mandate: to 'do good without losing money' (CDC Group, 2022). The state-owned company evolved over subsequent decades as the UK's relationship with its former empire changed, becoming the Commonwealth Development Corporation, then CDC Group, and since April 2022, British International Investment (BII). It has often invested through intermediary fund management companies and in 2004, as a part-privatisation for much of the investment management capacity of CDC Group at the time, the UK government even created its own 'spin-off' investment management company, Actis, which would operate as a 'commercially oriented fund' to pursue profits in the same way as other fund management companies (House of Commons International Development Committee, 2011).[8]

---

[8] The 'spin-off' of Actis, in which majority ownership was purchased by senior managers from within CDC Group, with the remaining 40 per cent held by the UK government, has been controversial. Members of an inquiry by the UK House of Commons described being 'astonished' to discover that managers from CDC Group collectively paid 'just £373,000' for their majority stake in Actis and that by 2010 'the taxpayer had not received any return despite being entitled to

In recent decades BII has expanded its investments in service sectors and its first investment in healthcare provision came in 2000, in the form of a USD 6.1 million investment in private South African healthcare chain, Prime Cure Clinics (CDC Group, 2001). The Prime Cure investment was revealing of a sentiment in the UK government, and the DFI community, that markets and business practices are an apparently pragmatic, even desirable, way to deliver services in social sectors. Prime Cure was described as a 'high quality, low cost alternative to the public health system' in South Africa (CDC Group, 2001, p. 11), and the investment came at a time when that public system was struggling with the ill-health caused by the HIV pandemic. Yet CDC Group's (as it was known then) involvement in healthcare provision would remain limited to Prime Cure for several years, and it was not until fund management companies began to take a stronger interest in the sector in the late 2000s that the DFI's own involvement grew. In 2007, Aureos Capital (a joint venture with Norway's DFI Norfund which was created in 2001 to support small and medium enterprises in low- and middle-income countries – CDC Group, 2001), invested USD 5.0 million of CDC Group money into Indian corporate chain Apollo to finance expansion of a flagship facility in Bangladesh. CDC Group also invested in the I-Ven Medicare fund created by India's ICICI to finance the burgeoning private healthcare provision sector in India (Singh, 2008). India would go on to become a focal point for CDC Group, with the DFI investing, indirectly or directly, in the expansion of a range of smaller, often single speciality private healthcare chains (Table 3).

A new organisational strategy in 2011 sought to reduce reliance on intermediary funds and enhance the developmental justification for CDC Group's work, emphasising job creation as a central tenet (Department for International Development, 2011). The company did continue its use of intermediary funds, but also made a series of *direct* investments in Indian healthcare providers: Rainbow, Narayana, CARE, Asian Institute of Medical Sciences and Dr Agarwal's Health Care. In the case of Dr Agarwal's Health Care, CDC's investment took it into collaboration with the healthcare company's majority owner – Singapore's sovereign wealth fund Temasek (see Section 7). CDC Group's involvement outside India grew too, using intermediary fund managers with a range of geographical foci: Takura (Southern Africa), Novastar (East Africa), XSML (Central Africa), and Mediterrania and Ezdehar (both Northern Africa) (CDC Group, 2021c). In 2015, CDC launched a joint venture with HealthCare Global (another recipient of investment from Singapore's Temasek)

---

80 per cent of the company's profits' (House of Commons International Development Committee, 2011, p. 25).

Table 3 CDC group / British investment international and India's private healthcare providers

Year of Investment	Healthcare Provider	Direct Investments — Size of Investment	Indirect Investments (via an intermediary) — Fund Manager, and Size and Year of CDC Group's Investment in Fund	Indirect Investments (via an intermediary) — Size of Fund's Investment in Provider
2007	Sahyadri Hospital		ICICI Venture I-Ven Medicare, USD 75 million, 2006	USD 36 million[1]
2007	Vikram Hospital			USD 24 million[1]
2007	Medica Synergy			USD 16 million[1]
2007	RG Stone			USD 10 million[1]
2010	BSR Super Speciality Hospital		Aureos, USD 35 million, 2006	USD 10 million[2]
2011	Vaatsalya		Seed Fund Advisory, USD 13 million, 2009	Portion of USD 10 million funding round[3]
2011	Mydentist (Sabka)			Unknown
2013	Rainbow Healthcare	USD 49 million	N/A	
2013	Vikram		Multiples Investment Advisers, USD 0.5 million, 2010	USD 30 million[4]
2014	Narayana Health	USD 50 million	N/A	
2014	Vaatsalya		Aavishkaar Venture Management Services, USD 25 million, 2011	Unknown

Table 3 (cont.)

Year of Investment	Healthcare Provider	Direct Investments	Indirect Investments (via an intermediary)	
		Size of Investment	Fund Manager, and Size and Year of CDC Group's Investment in Fund	Size of Fund's Investment in Provider
2014	Deep Chand Dialysis Centre (DCDC)		Pragati India Asset Management, USD 50 million, 2011	USD 5 million[5]
2016	CARE Hospitals	USD 30 million	N/A	
2016	Nu Cosmetic Clinic		Ambit Pragma Ventures, USD 20 million, 2008	Unknown
2017	Asian Institute of Medical Sciences	USD 21 million	N/A	
2017	Dr Mohan's Diabetes Specialities Centre		Lok Capital, USD 33 million, 2016	Portion of USD 10 million funding round[6]
2019	Dr Agarwal's Health Care	USD 31 million	N/A	
2019	Disha Medical Services		Swiss-Asia Financial Services, USD 15 million, 2015	Portion of USD 4 million funding round[7]
2019	Ayu Health Hospitals		Stellaris Advisors, USD 10 million, 2018	Portion of USD 6 million funding round[8]

Source: CDC Group's list of investments (CDC Group, 2021c) unless otherwise stated – 1. K. Singh (2008), 2. VCCircle (2010), 3. Abrar (2011), 4. Mint (2016), 5. Rai (2018), 6. Rajagopal (2017), 7. Medical Dialogues (2019), 8 The Economic Times (2021). Notes. Figures rounded to nearest million. Excludes home care, mobile health technologies and health insurance companies.

to establish a chain of oncology clinics in Africa, starting with the acquisition of Cancer Care Kenya (CDC Group, 2017). CDC Group was also one of the DFIs most exposed to potential loss when Abraaj's web of fraud began to unravel in 2019: CDC and Abraaj had developed a close relationship after the latter's acquisition of CDC Group spin-off Aureos in 2012 (Reuters, 2012) and almost USD 130 million in healthcare provision co-investments from CDC Group had followed (Rainbow Hospitals, Narayana Health and CARE Hospitals). So it came as no surprise that CDC Group then committed USD 50 million to join the IFC, USA Overseas Private Investment Corporation and Gates Foundation as one of the largest investors in Abraaj's flagship Growth Markets Health Fund, which since Abraaj's collapse has been managed by USA private equity firm TPG.

With the advent of calls to increase private finance in development in the 2010s, and for DFIs to co-invest and 'blend' their finance with that of private partners, CDC Group moved to occupy a leading role by positioning itself as an intellectual hub for 'impact investing'. UK government buy-in for this strategy was indicated by the hiring of Big Society Capital founder and former Gates Foundation blended finance advisor Nick O'Donohoe as CDC Group's new CEO in 2017 (Aldane, n.d.), accompanied by capital increases and growth of the number of staff in the DFI's Impact Team from 3 to 56 within two years (CDC Group & Department for International Development, 2019). The DFI has since produced a range of toolkits and instruments to document and examine investment impacts (CDC Group, 2019, 2021b), and was handed control of the UK government's IMPACT Programme to provide technical assistance to investors for working in this area (CDC Group, 2021a). CDC Group loaned USD 10 million to Amsterdam-based Stichting Medical Credit Fund – a provider of loans to healthcare companies in Africa – to support its attempts to demonstrate that private healthcare is 'bankable' and provides 'a reasonable return to investors' (PharmAccess Group, 2021, p. 5).

Although CDC Group's (and since 2021, BII's) developmental claims have largely focused on job creation, the rise of the language of impact investing has been accompanied by a search for wider claims of impact that can be made in the social sectors. One such claim reproduces thinking from the 1980s and 1990s about competition, suggesting that private healthcare (and education) might 'provide choice and raise standards' as a complement to public sector provision (UK Government, 2017). In other cases, the emphasis has been on pragmatism; that private services are the only way to expand healthcare provision in contexts of limited public resources. CDC Group sought to demonstrate the contribution of its investments to this endeavour through a dedicated toolkit which analyses healthcare providers' activities according to issues of quality, access, workforce and stewardship (Wadge et al., 2017b). It has also spearheaded the 'Investors for Health' initiative with the IFC, Dalberg and Quadria, where like-minded investors can discuss how to build 'inclusive healthcare systems in emerging markets' and avoid approaches that might '*inadvertently* undermine the goal of universal health coverage' (Investors for Health, 2021, emphasis added). The initiative seems to rely on interpretations of inclusivity and universal health coverage that permit substantial inequalities so long as the poorest groups receive some basic level of services.

Although for much of its recent history CDC Group tended to place less emphasis on the promotion of national interests in its work, favouring instead to emphasise job creation and a broader range of social impacts, this has been challenged through its rebranding as BII. For several years UK government policy has fixated on using the UK's development apparatus to advance domestic economic interests (HM Treasury, 2015), and leading politicians called for CDC Group to be part of this (Mawdsley, 2016). These pressures resulted in the merger of CDC Group's host government department, the Department for International Development, into the Foreign and Commonwealth Office in 2020. A strategy change for CDC Group followed in 2022, with notions of British imperialism resurrected through its rebranding as *British* (not UK) International Investment. The organisation could serve the Foreign, Commonwealth and Development Office by simultaneously advancing UK commercial interests while responding to perceived geopolitical threats from China. A leading minister called on BII to 'benefit the UK by creating opportunities in areas like project management, construction and clean energy' (UK Government, 2021) while helping to 'cement the UK as a development finance hub' (CDC Group, 2021d), with its 'clean, honest and reliable financing' offering an alternative to the financing from China which is presented as less desirable on these terms (UK Government, 2021).

France

In 2008, French DFI Proparco was embarking on a new phase of activity. Proparco is part-owned by private institutions, and in that year it raised EUR 300 million from its various investors, to provide the capital needed to fund an expansion in its geographical remit beyond one which had been based heavily on French empire, to now cover the whole of the Global South (Proparco, 2009). Its annual commitments had quadrupled in four years and were increasingly being described using language that would go on to become the mainstay of the Wall Street Consensus and the Addis Ababa Action Agenda: Proparco aimed to 'catalyse private investments in emerging and developing countries in order to support growth, sustainable development and the Millennium Development

Goals' (Proparco, 2009, p. 16). An updating of priority sectors for investment saw two social sectors, health and education, picked out as strategic targets. Earlier organisational publications had identified health as one of various relevant social development issues for Proparco, and indeed sectoral interest dated back at least as early as 2001 when a new director began advocating for greater priority to be afforded to healthcare (Guillon, 2021). But, reflecting some of the logics of CDC Group at the time, the 2008 strategy articulated an even stronger vision for social sector privatisation in which private organisations would 'become an intermediary for public policy by directly providing certain basic services in social sectors' (Proparco, 2009, p. 16).

Within a few years of its new strategy, Proparco had financial interests in the private healthcare systems of several countries, with many of those investments made through intermediary fund management companies. In 2009 Proparco invested USD 10 million in private fund manager Aureos' Africa Health Fund – an outcome of the IFC- and Gates Foundation–backed *Business of Health in Africa* initiative. A few years later, in 2014, Proparco invested USD 15 million in an Abraaj fund aiming to develop a chain of private hospitals across North Africa (Proparco, 2014c). Germany's DEG and the European Bank for Reconstruction and Development were the other investors in that USD 200 million fund, as it quickly built up a chain of hospitals within Egypt and Tunisia (RMBV, 2021). Proparco also committed USD 10 million to Abraaj's Growth Markets Health Fund in conjunction with several national and multilateral DFIs (Global Justice Now, 2020), while in Asia it invested USD 15 million in a Quadria fund (Proparco, 2015c) which went on to purchase equity in private hospitals in Vietnam, India and Indonesia (Quadria Capital, 2021).

In other cases Proparco used loans to support private healthcare expansion. In Tunisia, Proparco provided a USD 6 million loan to finance construction of the country's first private cancer clinic – Clinique Internationale Med Hannibal (Proparco, 2009); in Lebanon, USD 15 million for construction of two hospitals so CareMed could pursue plans to become Lebanon's top private healthcare group (Proparco, 2013); in Brazil, USD 35 million to support upgrading and expansion of two private hospitals (Proparco, 2011; Sirio-Libanes Hospital, 2014), and in Dominican Republic, USD 10 million for the modernisation of the country's largest facility – Hospital Metropolitano de Santiago (Proparco, 2014a). Chains of hospitals were also offered support to facilitate their enlargement: USD 62 million for the Rede D'Or chain in Brazil (as part of a USD 250 million IFC-brokered package) (IFC, 2014b); and USD 25 million to Georgia's Evex to capitalise on healthcare privatisation reforms in the country (Proparco, 2016a). The intensity of activity in that period, from 2009 to the mid-2010s, saw Proparco invest in the expansion of private hospitals and healthcare chains across three continents.

Proparco's pursuit of healthcare investments was initially justified by the organisation on a social basis: ensuring the provision of 'basic services' to people who needed them (Proparco, 2009). The idea was that private provision could 'complement' public services 'without any significant risk of supplanting them or undermining the social equilibrium' (Proparco, 2006, p. 20). It is a positive sums claim that assumes the healthcare system benefits as a whole from private healthcare provision to wealthier groups, as healthcare becomes 'accessible to as many people as possible' (Renault & Rousselot, 2013, p. 12). However, that questionable logic slipped from view within just a few years of the 2008 strategy, as organisational materials lost their emphasis on complementing basic services and switched to the language of marketisation; the idea was that the private sector could make healthcare systems 'more efficient' in light of 'inadequate' public healthcare (Proparco, 2013, p. 21), and that 'world-class private healthcare services' were needed to ensure 'better healthcare' within countries (Proparco, 2015a). By 2015, when Proparco announced a new strategy with plans to increase health and education to 7 per cent of its total portfolio, the organisation's publications and media releases stopped setting out social justifications for healthcare.

Instead Proparco's investment strategy appears, implicitly at least, to revolve around making investments that are most valuable from a commercial, rather than social, perspective: funding the expansion of corporate chains that serve the healthcare needs of middle-class consumers in middle-income countries. In recent years it has made investments of USD 5 million in African healthcare chain CIEL (Proparco, 2015b); USD 9 million in East African chain AAR Healthcare (Proparco, 2018); and USD 20 million to support expansion of a diagnostic services chain in the Middle East (Proparco, 2019). In 2020 Proparco announced a USD 20 million equity investment in Humania – an equity fund created by the founder of Saudi-German Hospitals – as part of a USD 360 million finance package involving the IFC, European Bank for Reconstruction and Development and DFIs from Finland and Denmark (Proparco, 2020). The stated aims of the consortium are to build a chain of facilities that will improve access to healthcare for 1 million people in Egypt and Morocco, but Saudi-German Hospitals have a strong focus on wealthy and international healthcare users, and Humania's website only vaguely claims the chain will 'improve wellbeing' alongside a more compelling offer of 'strong returns for our investors' (Humania, 2022).

Commercial value and economic returns also appear to have been central to Proparco's recent involvement in Turkey's integrated health campus projects.

Announced by the Turkish government in 2010 (IFC, 2015), and part of a reform programme that began in 2003 (Yilmaz, 2017), the integrated health campuses are intended to modernise and expand Turkey's public healthcare system and to strengthen Turkey's position as a regional and global healthcare hub (Cumhuriyet, 2011). The Turkish government opted for a 'public-private partnership' financing model (also sometimes referred to as 'private finance initiative') for construction of the hospitals: a private consortium raises funds to build the infrastructure, which then passes into public ownership while the consortium is repaid by the commissioning government over the subsequent 20–30 years. What is most striking about Turkey's integrated health campus initiative, aside from the scale of the debts being incurred (USD 11.6 billion in upfront costs alone – Government of Turkey, 2021) is that much of this debt is owed to, or guaranteed by, investor states whose national champion companies participate in the construction consortia. In the case of France this is Meridiam, affectionately referred to in one Proparco document as 'France's No. 1 infrastructure fund' (Proparco, 2017).[9] Between 2014 and 2017, Proparco committed almost USD 100 million to health campus projects involving Meridiam, in Adana, Elazig and Bursa (Proparco, 2014b, 2016b, 2017), and Meridiam, like other companies in the construction consortia, stands to benefit significantly from project contracts. France benefits from the returnable investments and accompanying interest payments (reports from other health campuses indicate expected returns in the region of 7–9 per cent – Cho, 2014; D. Kim, 2018), as well as from Meridiam's commercial success and its contribution to the French economy. Like the UK and BII, France and Proparco appear to be placing greater emphasis on commercial considerations in a context of economic nationalism and financialised logics for development financing.

5 Sweden, Netherlands and Development Finance Institutions

For some states and their DFIs, the fusion of national economic concerns and claimed development objectives has been overt for some time. In this section I consider the activities of Sweden and the Netherlands, two states whose DFIs have placed substantial emphasis on serving domestic business interests. Though not quite as wide-reaching in their private healthcare investments as compared to the UK and France, their involvement has nonetheless been important in specific contexts. Like their European counterparts, they are

---

[9] In a contribution to the 2015 G20 meeting report, Meridiam lauded the controversial public-private partnership model as 'efficient, cost-effective and offer[ing] great value for money', making a rather unfortunately worded call for other organisations to 'feed on' projects like Turkey's health campuses (The G20 Research Group, 2015, pp. 120–21).

becoming stakeholders in corporate healthcare provision in low- and middle-income countries.

Sweden

Swedfund, the national DFI of Sweden, was created in 1979 with the aim of financing the expansion of manufacturing industries in Global South countries to encourage economic growth (Swedfund, 2020a). In that, it matched the vision of older bilateral DFIs such as BII, but Swedfund originally operated as a foundation and it was not until 1991 that the Swedish government transformed it into a state-owned company to encourage a more commercial (returns-driven) approach to investment. Unlike some other DFIs, Swedfund has long had an explicitly nationalist thrust to its work, with an explicit aim 'to promote Swedish interests' (Swedfund, 2020a, p. 75). In practice this has meant promoting Swedish *business* interests: 'cooperation' with Swedish companies has been listed as one of three goals for Swedfund (the other two being 'development' and 'profitability'), with particular emphasis on promoting 'internationalisation and expansion onto new markets' for Swedish companies (Swedfund, 2010b, p. 4).

It was Swedfund's interest in promoting Swedish business interests overseas that led to its first investment in healthcare provision, with Swedish medical technology company Elekta. In 1999, Elekta announced plans to establish a Gamma Knife Center in Egypt, named after Elekta's world-renowned 'Gamma Knife' radiosurgery technology. Since its first clinical testing in 1968 in Stockholm's private Sophiahemmet Hospital, the Gamma Knife had become a commercial success in high-income settings, but by the late-1990s Elekta was posting what its President admitted were 'highly unsatisfactory [financial] results' (Elekta, 1999, p. 4). This was due in part to weakening demand for its products in Europe and parts of Asia, and the company looked to greater penetration in new markets as key for its future growth (Elekta, 1999). The Cairo Gamma Knife Center would end up at the forefront of those efforts.

The Gamma Knife Center was designed as a joint venture between Elekta, Swedish medical consultancy Scandinavian Care Projects and, unusually, the Swedish government's DFI Swedfund. Swedfund's contribution to the Cairo Gamma Knife Center was relatively small compared to DFI investments that have taken place since – a commitment of USD 0.8 million in equity investment and loans (Swedfund, 2010a) – but it was the first time a national DFI had invested in healthcare provision like this. Other bilateral DFIs had, up until this point, shown little interest in private healthcare provision and the opportunities it presented for domestic companies. The Egyptian government also invested in the joint venture through the National Bank of Egypt (Oxford Business Group, n.d.), and agreed for the Gamma Knife Center to be set up within the site of prestigious public healthcare institution, the Nasser Institute for Research and Treatment. The intention for Swedfund and Elekta was not only to expand Elekta's presence within Egypt, but regionally (Elekta, 2001); indeed, by the end of the 2000s, Elekta's sales growth in the Middle East was outpacing that in Europe.

Swedfund's initial foray into healthcare provision with Elekta was followed up with a series of other investments in the sector. In 2006, Swedfund invested USD 1.1 million in Addis Cardiac Hospital, a private facility set up by a Swedish cardiologist living in Ethiopia (Ethiopia Observer, 2018), followed by an unspecified equity investment and loan for KurdMed eye hospital in Iraq (2008). But it was Elekta which was the focus of attention and the perceived success its clinic in Cairo saw that become the first in a series of joint investments by Swedfund and Elekta (Swedfund, 2012). In 2009, ten years on from the initial Gamma Knife Center agreement, Swedfund and Elekta jointly established their own investment fund – Global Medical Investments – which would finance the construction of a wave of new Gamma Knife clinics in different regions. By this time the Global Financial Crisis was well underway, and governments were facing pressure to support domestic businesses through an economic downturn. Swedfund invested USD 9 million in Global Medical Investments and took a 48 per cent stake in the investment fund, with Elekta taking another 48 per cent stake (Swedfund, 2013a). Scandinavian Care Projects also benefitted, through contracts to repeat the work it had performed in Egypt (Scandinavian Care, 2021). The Swedish government's support did not end there: state-owned company Svensk Exportkredit [Swedish Export Credit] and private banks from Sweden provided additional financial capital to build the clinics (Swedfund, 2012), and the private lenders' loans were guaranteed against losses by the government's Exportkreditnämnden [Export Credits Board]. Even the Swedish Prime Minister was drafted into action, speaking at the inauguration of a Gamma Knife Center in Chile (Swedfund, 2012). Global Medical Investments expanded quickly, and within a few years they had launched clinics in Chile, Ecuador, Dominican Republic, Ghana, Indonesia and Mexico.

During the past decade, developmental justifications have become more prominent in Swedfund's work, reflecting the growing influence of ideas around 'impact investing' amongst DFIs (see Section 4). A new organisational strategy for Swedfund was introduced in 2012, placing more emphasis on poverty reduction through business expansion and job creation and the following year a USD 4 million investment in Nairobi Women's Hospital (which had already received investment from Africa Health Fund) was justified on this basis (Swedfund, 2014). At the same time, claims that investments would expand access to healthcare were also becoming more visible, for example in the stated justifications for a USD 3 million investment in AAR Clinics (Kenya, with co-investors the IFC and the Investment Fund for Health in Africa) (IFC, 2013), and an investment in Medica Synergie (India, with DEG and Quadria) (Gooptu, 2013). In the case of Global Medical Investments and its Gamma Knife Centers, user fees paid by wealthy groups were expected to subsidise fees for poorer groups 'who would otherwise have no access to treatment' (Swedfund, 2013a, p. 42), although the extent to which the kind of cross-subsidy takes place is unclear.

By 2018, and the launch of Swedfund's latest strategy, the health sector had been made a priority area for the organisation's investments, alongside energy and financial services, and with particular focus areas of healthcare, pharmaceuticals and e-health. This has since seen Swedfund invest in a suite of health-focused intermediary fund managers: Hospital Holdings Investment and Medical Credit Fund in Africa, and HealthQuad and Quadria in India (Swedfund, 2022). The aim is 'to ensure that everyone has access to healthcare and medicines in developing countries' (Swedfund, 2020a, p. 28), though this seems to rest on the same narrow interpretation of universality adopted by other DFIs when trying to reconcile their developmental mandates with the inequalities fostered by corporate healthcare expansion. The tension was illustrated by Swedfund's recent investment in Kenya's Jacaranda Maternity: a company 'spun out' from Jacaranda Health, a non-profit organisation created by a former impact investor, when its owners realised the limited scope for expansion and the need for the hospital 'to act more like a business and less like a nonprofit' (Pearson, 2022). After hiring a former financier to be CEO of the hospital, and attracting investment from Swedfund, Johnson & Johnson's philanthropic foundation, and fund manager Asia Africa Investment and Consulting, the hospital now pursues 'a vision to become the region's leading provider of safe and affordable maternal care within ten years' (Swedfund, 2020b).

Overt domestic economic interests appear to have been downgraded from Swedfund's work, in contrast to changes taking place at BII, Proparco and the FMO (next section). Statements point to the continued relevance of Swedfund for Swedish business, such as how Swedfund 'mitigates the overall risk faced by private-sector companies investing in the most challenging developing countries' (Swedfund, 2013b, p. 11) and how it can fund feasibility studies that create commercial opportunities 'for Swedish companies which offer sustainable and long-term profitable solutions' (Swedfund, 2020a, p. 38).

Indeed, its Swedpartnership programme continues to support small- and medium-sized Swedish businesses to 'establish an operation in developing countries' (Swedfund, 2020a). Meanwhile the experience of Global Medical Investments is lauded as an example of how Swedfund can open healthcare systems up to Swedish companies 'with relatively developed products where it is important to find new markets' (Swedfund, 2013a, p. 42).

In recent moves indicative of pressures on investors to maintain perpetual motion (repeatedly seeking out opportunities for growth, investing, adding value and then selling and moving on), Global Medical Investments has begun selling its stakes in select Gamma Knife Centers. In 2020 Global Medical Investments sold its Ecuador clinic to American Shared Hospital Services for USD 2.0 million in a deal financed by the latter using loans from the USA's International Development Finance Corporation and described by the American Shared Hospital Services' CEO as bringing 'an additional revenue stream for future growth' (Financial Times, 2020). This was then followed in 2021 by the sale of Global Medical Investments' Ghana clinic, this time for an undisclosed sum to teaching union Ghana National Association of Teachers (Ghana National Association of Teachers, 2021). The union already had an agreement in place with the clinic to provide cancer care to its members, and its purchase of the clinic appears to be an attempt to pre-empt acquisition by parties who might pursue alternative business models and jeopardise access to the clinic's services. It is symptomatic of an industry where claims of universalism are undermined by limited rights of access and the financialised logics of owners.

Netherlands

Founded in 1970, the Dutch FMO has pursued a broad mission of supporting business expansion and economic growth in the Global South, but with particular interest in specific sectors, including the financial services sector (FMO, 1998, 2005), and more recently energy and agribusiness (including water) (FMO, 2012, 2020a). The DFI is 51 per cent state-owned and 49 per cent privately owned, primarily by Dutch commercial banks but also with small shareholdings held by business associations, trade unions and individual investors (FMO, 2022b). The private interests within the FMO have become more overt in guiding its activities since the early 2010s when, as part of a combined 'aid and trade' agenda for the Dutch government (Wemos, 2020), a new strategy for FMO introduced the idea of 'increasing Dutch [business] interest' in 'development markets' (FMO, 2013, p. 24). This was operationalised in various ways: the FMO was handed control of a Dutch government programme Fonds

Opkomende Markten OntwikkelingsSamenwerking [Emerging Markets Development Cooperation Fund] which provided financial support to Dutch companies looking to expand in so-called 'emerging markets'; set up the 'NL Business' department to organise its networking efforts amongst Dutch companies (FMO, 2015a, p. 21) transferring those activities to a new FMO subsidiary called NedLinx in 2017 (FMO, 2019) and then Invest International in 2021 (see later in this section); and added 'increase Dutch business' to its list of organisational priorities (FMO, 2016).

Health has not been a priority sector for the FMO in the same way it has for some other DFIs, but the organisation's interest in bringing together and supporting Dutch business has drawn it into making healthcare investments. The first came in 2008, when FMO joined with several private investors and the African Development Bank to capitalise a new investment fund aiming to channel financing into Africa's private healthcare sector – Investment Fund for Health in Africa (Doherty, 2011; IFC, 2014a). The Amsterdam-based fund brings together Dutch business interests across multiple sectors: it was established by two senior managers from Dutch non-governmental organisation PharmAccess, and received financing from Dutch pension fund Algemene Pensioen Groep and the Stichting Social Investor Foundation for Africa, which itself combines grants from corporations, including several headquartered in the Netherlands – financial services companies Achmea and SNS-Reaal, life insurance company AEGON and alcohol company Heineken. The FMO invested USD 15 million initially, but such was the perceived success of the fund that it later committed another USD 24 million to a second funding round, this time in conjunction with the IFC, European Investment Bank and Achmea (FMO, 2015b), and the Dutch Good Growth Fund – a government programme created in 2014 to boost investment and exports by Dutch companies in the Global South (OECD, 2016). This has been accompanied by investment in PharmAccess' Medical Credit Fund, which provides loans to healthcare providers in Africa to procure equipment and pharmaceuticals and to expand (Medical Credit Fund, 2014), and which received a second round of funding from FMO, and from the Dutch Ministry of Foreign Affairs, in 2021 (Medical Credit Fund, 2021).

The FMO's involvement in initiatives like the Investment Fund for Health in Africa has been justified by drawing attention to potential developmental benefits in the form of 'employment and the access to quality healthcare' (FMO, 2015c), echoing the kinds of claims made by other DFIs. But like the investments made by those DFIs, FMO and Investment Fund for Health in Africa appear to be focused on financing the growth of private healthcare providers. The fund has invested in AAR in Kenya, Kampala Hospital and

Nakasero Hospital in Uganda, Hygeia in Nigeria, and CIEL in Uganda and Mauritius (Investment Fund for Health in Africa, 2022). In each case the aim of investment was to finance expansion of these private providers through the construction or acquisition of new facilities. In the case of Hygeia, FMO provided additional capital for growth in the form of a further loan provided in 2009, as part of a combined USD 25 million investment with the IFC and private equity firm Satya Capital to support Hygeia's vision of becoming a hub for medical tourism in Western Africa (Satya Capital, 2009). Meanwhile the benefits of Investment Fund for Health in Africa to Dutch business, and in particular the Dutch financial services industry, are pronounced. Indeed, a director of corporate social responsibility from Achmea has been frank on the business case for investment: 'Not only does our investment in IFHA [Investment Fund for Health in Africa] generate a healthy profit, it ensures we can contribute to accessible, affordable and quality healthcare in Africa. This makes it a classic example of profit with purpose' (FMO, 2015c).

But it is the Dutch government's relationship with Amsterdam-headquartered technology giant Philips which has drawn the Dutch state most extensively into the healthcare provision sector as an investor. Philips has been a beneficiary of Dutch export credit and 'tied aid' contracts in Africa for at least twenty years, allowing it to embed its technologies within healthcare settings and create opportunities for longer-term maintenance contracts (Wemos, 2019). Plans for growth in the aftermath of the Global Financial Crisis emphasised the need to pursue 'emerging markets' (Philips, 2010, p. 100), and the company picked out the African continent for specific attention, developing an 'aggressive multiyear investment plan' (Philips, 2013a) in a region where the FMO and organisations such as the IFC and Gates Foundation had been so keen to stress the potential for private sector growth and investment (IFC, 2008b). Philips launched an annual 'Africa roadshow' in 2010, and shortly after the third iteration of the roadshow in 2012, the company launched a Fabric of Africa programme – an initiative to introduce public-private 'partnerships' that would encourage technological solutions to improve primary healthcare; the name came from a claimed interest in fostering healthy women, who were designated the 'fabric' of Africa (Philips, 2013b). Philips partnered with FMO-recipient Medical Credit Fund in 2014, in a deal lauded by the Dutch Minister for Foreign Trade and Development Cooperation, offering Medical Credit Fund financing to healthcare facilities in Ghana, Kenya, Nigeria and Tanzania to help them pay for Philips' technologies and services (Medical Credit Fund, 2014). It then partnered with the avowedly entrepreneurial non-governmental organisation African Medical and Research Foundation (Philips, 2015b), and established a Kenya 'innovation hub' to develop 'locally relevant solutions' to healthcare issues in the continent

(Philips, 2015a). They quickly developed a range of agreements to supply Africa's governmental and non-governmental organisations with healthcare technologies, maintenance and training services.

The Dutch government was soon enrolled in the advancement of Philips' agenda for Africa as part of the former's push for Dutch healthcare exports to the continent. In 2016, the Dutch embassy in Kenya, with support from Dutch industry network Task Force Health Care, commissioned a study to identify commercial opportunities in Kenya for Dutch life sciences and healthcare companies (Task Force Health Care & Kenya Healthcare Federation, 2016). Philips featured prominently in the report's interviews and case studies, having already signed contracts with the Kenyan government to equip hospitals in several provinces, as well as having launched its first Community Life Center, in Kiambu. The Community Life Center model, which Philips subsequently expanded to another province in Kenya and to Democratic Republic of Congo, involved development of a building that integrates Philips' technologies for electricity and lighting, water purification, and diagnostics, and which is proposed by the company as a solution to the lack of access to primary healthcare and other basic services in Africa (Philips, 2016).

The following year, in 2017, the Dutch embassy in Kenya commissioned another report, this time looking at the ability of Kenya's health ministry to 'fast track' public-private partnerships in primary healthcare (Rijksdienst voor Ondernemend Nederland, 2017). The report was timed to coincide with a Dutch healthcare trade mission to Kenya (Task Force Health Care, 2017), and reflected Philips' interest in positioning itself as a provider of primary healthcare solutions for Africa. Interviews conducted by Dutch non-governmental organisation Wemos (2020) indicate this second report by the embassy was commissioned following a request from the Kenyan government's SDG Partnership Platform (Government of Kenya, 2019); the SDG Partnership Platform's two donors at that time were Philips and the Dutch Ministry of Foreign Affairs (UNDP, 2021). Political support from the Dutch government sought to create the right policy environment, but the financial costs for Philips' expansion posed another potential barrier, creating an opportunity for FMO involvement.

The FMO's direct support for Philips in Africa began with financing from a Business Development Accelerator, which aims to support Dutch businesses in early-stage 'development of bankable projects in emerging markets' in agri-food, water, health and climate sectors (FMO, 2020b). Through this, the FMO committed an initial EUR 200,000 to a joint 'Partnership for Primary Care' project between African Medical and Research Foundation and Philips which saw the former take over management of primary healthcare facilities, and the latter equipping them (African Medical and Research Foundation, 2022). It was a pilot project in three facilities described by the FMO as seeking to 'demonstrate that the outsourcing of the management of public primary healthcare facilities to the private sector leads to better health results' (FMO, 2020b, p. 11). The perceived success of the arrangement saw it scaled up to 233 facilities in Makueni County using another EUR 1 million from the Development Accelerator. Other Philips projects supported by FMO using the Development Accelerator include EUR 0.8 million for the upgrading of healthcare facilities in Republic of Congo, and EUR 0.3 million to support the feasibility study for a private hospital and nursing/medical college in Bangladesh, in the expectation that Philips would benefit from the subsequent construction contracts (FMO, 2021a).

The ultimate goal for FMO and Philips in Africa appears to be regional dominance. The current phase of work in Kenya aims to culminate in pitching the Kenyan government a plan for nationwide adoption of Philips' outsourcing model for public primary healthcare (FMO, 2020b), something that the Dutch government and Philips are well placed to do given their influence in the SDG Partnership Platform and through the Dutch embassy's work. The FMO and Philips recently signed a five-year partnership agreement to trial primary healthcare innovations in Africa, 'to develop projects from ideation to proof of concept' (Philips, 2021). Citing the importance of achieving 'universal health coverage', they have agreed to invest up to EUR 1 million in each of around ten projects as they seek to produce primary care models that are 'investable at scale' (Philips, 2021).

Dutch investor state interest in healthcare was recently formalised, in 2021, with the launch of Invest International. A joint venture between the Ministry of Finance and the FMO, and partner organisation to a domestically focused Invest-NL, Invest International offers equity investments, loans and grants to de-risk the international expansion of Dutch businesses into low- and middle-income countries if a case for development impact can be made (FMO, 2021b). It aims to provide a single point of entry for this kind of work, bringing together activities previously performed by Rijksdienst voor Ondernemend Nederland [Netherlands Enterprise Agency] and FMO (including through NL Business / NedLinx), and formally wedding Dutch economic interests to a development mandate through its two strategic objectives: 'to contribute to the future earning capacity of the Netherlands, and to create impact on the Sustainable Development Goals' (Invest International, 2022). It offers support to private companies but also to government infrastructure projects in cases where 'the Dutch business community can play a role' (FMO, 2022a, p. 64), in other words looking to foster the kinds of public-private partnerships pursued by Philips.

Healthcare, a sector 'in which the business community in the Netherlands has a lot to offer', has been identified as one of its five focal areas for investment with Philips' public-private partnerships in Kenya held up as a success story for emulation (FMO, 2021b).

6 Japan, South Korea and National Development Banks

Applying the lens of 'investor state' in the study of healthcare provision encourages perspectives that go beyond the Anglo-European DFI activities described in Sections 4 and 5. In this section, the first of two on other forms of state investment, I show how Japan[10] and South Korea have used a combination of national development banks and export credit agencies to invest in overseas private healthcare projects. The aim of these investments is to secure lucrative contracts for national champion companies, resembling the activities of some European DFIs but with financial commitments far larger in size.

Japan

In 1999, the Japanese government launched a new agency, Japan Bank for International Cooperation (JBIC), created through the merger of its Overseas Economic Cooperation Fund and the Export-Import Bank of Japan. The Overseas Economic Cooperation Fund had been one of two Japanese agencies (with Japan International Cooperation Agency – JICA) tasked with administering the country's large development aid budget; the Export-Import Bank of Japan was a state agency used to subsidise and de-risk Japanese exports as part of Japan's developmental state model for economic development (C. Johnson, 1982). The formation of JBIC was argued to be necessary to rationalise Japanese support for public *and* private sectors in other countries in the aftermath of the Asian financial crisis (Nishigaki, 2000), but it also appeared to respond to pressure from a powerful Ministry of International Trade and Industry (now part of the Ministry of Economy, Trade and Industry) which had, in the context of a prolonged domestic recession, been pushing for Japanese industrial interests to be better represented in the spending of the development aid budget (Katada, 2002). Over subsequent years the expression

---

[10] Investor state activities by Japan have been largely channelled through the Japan Bank for International Cooperation, which is often referred to as a national development bank (Kring & Gallagher, 2019), but which is also sometimes included within lists and analyses of DFIs (Savoy et al., 2016), and sometimes omitted (OECD, 2022a). Japan Bank for International Cooperation has a mandate that encompasses overseas development and offers many of the same financing instruments as DFIs, but its origins lie in a developmental state context, it has strong domestic growth objectives and it incorporates export credit agency functions.

of domestic interests in JBIC's activities has become more overt, with the bank's stated mission now couched in ideas and terms relating to the political and economic security of Japan, and the interests of Japanese business (JBIC, 2019, p. 2).

Interest in pursuing domestic economic interests through investments in overseas healthcare providers emerged in the early 2010s. The Japanese government produced its Japan Revitalization Strategy in 2012 to revive a flagging national economy, earmarking healthcare as one of four priority areas. The economic interest in healthcare was primarily domestic, but the strategy also set out ambitions to expand healthcare exports including medical products and healthcare infrastructure. In this it reinforced attempts underway since 2011 to organise the industries exporting Japanese healthcare through a new non-profit association, Medical Excellence Japan. The aim set out in the Japan Revitalization Strategy was to extend these attempts using the aid, trade and diplomatic apparatus of the state – JICA, JBIC, Japan External Trade Organization and diplomatic missions – to 'promote global deployment of Japanese medical technologies and services' (Government of Japan, 2013, p. 95). This was then reiterated in a suite of new healthcare policies published in 2014 (Government of Japan, 2014, pp. 21–22), and underscored with the creation of the government's Task Force on International Expansion of Medical Businesses. The Ministry of Economy, Trade and Industry had already set about promoting Japanese healthcare interests abroad by contracting Medical Excellence Japan to conduct research and trade missions in Asian countries (Medical Excellence Japan, 2019).

The first successful deployment of this new strategy was in India. In 2012, Japanese companies Toyota Tsusho (part of conglomerate Toyota Group) and medical services firm Secom were collaborating with Indian engineering firm Kirloskar to construct a private general hospital in Bangalore under the name Sakra World Hospital (Business Standard, 2014). JBIC, newly tasked with financing such ventures, invested USD 10.7 million with the stated aim of 'maintaining and strengthening the international competitiveness of Japanese industries' (JBIC, 2014). Promotional materials emphasised the value of transferring Japanese healthcare knowledge and technologies to India, promoting high-quality healthcare to meet the needs of a growing middle-class population (Toyota Tsusho, 2016); however, the prominent 'international patients' section on the hospital's website suggests a wider audience for its services (Sakra World Hospital, 2022). The hospital was planned to be the first of several, with the venture aiming to build bed capacity of 20,000, but in 2016 Kirloskar sold its stake in the joint venture, amidst reports of tensions between the Indian and Japanese partners, leaving Sakra as India's first fully foreign-owned private hospital (Das, 2016).

Turkey's public-private partnership integrated health campuses (see Section 4) became a focal point for Japanese government interest in the sector. In 2014, aid agency JICA commissioned a feasibility study for a health campus planned for Aydın, but which had yet to go to tender. The intention was to develop a detailed plan of the planned campus project so that Japanese companies could bid for contracts, and JICA even proposed using its Private Sector Investment Fund to loan Turkey the upfront financing that would be needed to pay for the construction contracts (JICA, 2015). JICA also commissioned another feasibility study to look at an additional eight health campus projects which had not yet been tendered. The report identified five campuses as top targets for Japanese companies to bid for, again proposing to use JICA's Private Sector Investment Fund to provide the necessary financing (JICA, 2016, p. 200). At the time of writing, however, none of the untendered health campus projects identified in JICA's studies have advanced (Government of Turkey, 2021).

In the end it was serendipity that landed Japan one of Turkey's health campus projects. The flagship Ikitelli health campus in Istanbul, which had already been awarded to a consortium of Turkey's Emsaş İnşaat, USA-based Allen Shariff and Spain-based Forcimsa, had encountered problems when the consortium found itself unable to raise the necessary financial capital to proceed (InfraPPP, 2015). The project was instead handed to Turkish construction company Rönesans and Japanese technology company Sojitz (Sojitz, 2017). The two companies had collaborated previously on construction projects, but this was their first time working together in the healthcare sector. It was virgin territory and a project that would be technically demanding – Istanbul's health campus was not only envisaged as a vast complex with several hospital buildings and 2,700 beds, but also had to incorporate substantial earthquake-proofing due to the seismic history of Istanbul (Ikitelli Integrated Health Campus Project, 2016). The total upfront cost was USD 1.5 billion.

When it came to finding upfront financing for the Ikitelli project, the consortium diverged from other projects which often relied heavily on European development banks and DFIs, and instead used funds sourced entirely from Japanese institutions. JBIC provided loans exceeding USD 700 million (JBIC, 2017), approximately half the required funds, while further upfront financing was sourced through loans from a suite of private Japanese financial institutions: Sumitomo Mitsui, Nippon Life, Mitsubishi UFJ, Standard Chartered, Dai-ichi Life and Iyo Bank (JBIC, 2017). The Japanese government's Nippon Export and Investment Insurance company provided insurance for these private investors, while JBIC provided additional 'political risk guarantees' to protect the investors against losses that might be incurred by political crises like the 2016 failed coup.

Two years later, in another display of financial clout, JBIC provided USD 400 million in loans so that Japanese conglomerate Mitsui could increase its shareholding in hospital chain Integrated Healthcare Holdings (IHH) Berhad. IHH is one of the world's largest hospital providers with infrastructure spanning Singapore, Malaysia, Indonesia, India, China, Brunei, Vietnam, Turkey and North Macedonia, and at an initial public offering of shares in 2012 it was valued at USD 8 billion, second only to USA-based HCA amongst healthcare providers globally (Ngui & Kok, 2012). It also has a complex history of state involvement in its ownership (see Section 7), but that did not deter JBIC working with private investors to collectively provide loans totalling USD 1 billion to Mitsui, to increase its shareholding in IHH from 17 per cent to 33 per cent.

The loans, insurance and guarantees offered by JBIC and other institutions of the Japanese state reflect a longer history of support for a set of large national champion companies known as 'sogo shosha'. The rationale for JBIC's support for Mitsui's stake in IHH was simple: JBIC 'supported the expansion of Mitsui's business overseas in the healthcare sector' (JBIC, 2021, p. 3). Meanwhile Sojitz's involvement in the Ikitelli project would provide immediate financial benefits to the company and also serve as a demonstration project to pitch for future contracts. The company has created a Medical Infrastructure Department to implement its vision as a leader in hospital construction (Sojitz, 2020b), and Ikitelli has been lauded by Sojitz as a resounding success which was not only completed ahead of schedule, but also opened prior to completion at the request of the Turkish government in order to host people being treated for coronavirus disease (COVID-19) (Sojitz, 2020a). The scale of financial support provided by the Japanese state to these sogo shosha is unsurprising given the history of developmentalism in the country, but what is now apparent is that this is extending on a large scale into the social sectors of other countries.

South Korea

The financing apparatus used by South Korea in overseas private healthcare projects reflects its own history of developmentalism. Korea Development Bank was founded in 1954 to finance re-construction in the aftermath of the Korean War largely using development aid from the USA (K. Lee, 2019), but over subsequent decades took on a broader domestic mandate as financer for South Korea's emerging export industries. Its work was complemented by the Export-Import Bank of Korea, created in 1976 to support exports and which has a stated mission to contribute to the 'national economy' of South Korea (Export-Import Bank of Korea, 2021). It is only in recent years that the Korea

Development Bank has been given a wider geographic remit to invest in other countries in order to create opportunities for South Korean companies (J. Kim, 2015). At the same time, the South Korean government has taken a stronger interest in supporting domestic companies to access the large contracts that come with building or equipping overseas healthcare systems. Like Japan, until the 2010s South Korea's healthcare exports were geared more towards inward medical tourism and the export of medical products and technologies, encouraged by a Korea Health Industry Development Institute created by the Ministry of Health in 1999 (Lunt, 2017). The convergence of these two developments – a financing apparatus tasked with supporting domestic exports and a healthcare sector looking for opportunities in a fast-growing global healthcare economy – set the foundations for South Korea's recent emergence as an investor state in the sector.

In 2016, Korea Development Bank and the Export-Import Bank of Korea announced that they would be financing the construction of an integrated health campus in Gaziantep, one of Turkey's largest cities, situated near the Turkey-Syria border. Gaziantep's health campus was envisaged as a grand complex comprising a city hospital, psychiatric hospital and rehabilitation hospital, totalling nearly 2,000 beds (Gaziantep Special Purpose Vehicle, 2021). The total cost for the project was expected to be USD 750 million (The Korea Times, 2012), and key investors included the European Bank for Reconstruction and Development, the European Investment Bank and public and private South Korean banks. Unlike the European banks, the South Korean state had no previous involvement in the integrated health campus initiative, but the involvement of South Korean conglomerate Samsung gave a strong economic incentive for participation. The consortium that had been awarded the construction tender for Gaziantep comprised Samsung, Turkish construction firm Kayi and Italian industrial group Salini Impregilo (now Webuild) (The Korea Times, 2012). Samsung's contribution came through the expertise and services offered by subsidiaries Samsung C&T (construction and engineering) and Samsung Life Insurance (financial services) (Cho, 2014), and Samsung Asset Management, part of Samsung Life Insurance, was tasked with organising the necessary financing. Samsung stood to receive USD 180 million for its part in the work (The Korea Times, 2012).

The importance of Samsung's lucrative Gaziantep contract to the South Korean state is indicated by the lengths to which the South Korean government went to ensure upfront financing for the project could be found. State-owned Korea Development Bank invested in the Gaziantep project through its subsidiary KDB Infrastructure Investments Asset Management Co. (KIAMCO), which pools together public and private financing to make investments; in this case USD 67 million in loans for the Gaziantep project. The South Korean government also provided loans of USD 80 million using its Export-Import Bank of Korea (InfraPPP, 2017), and used two export credit agencies to protect the investments made by public and private creditors from Korea: Export-Import Bank of Korea provided USD 80 million in loan guarantees, while Korea Trade Insurance Corporation provided loan guarantees totalling USD 160 million (Hospital Management, 2017). Gaziantep was reportedly the first time that the Export-Import Bank of Korea had been used to secure an overseas hospital construction contract for a South Korean company (InfraPPP, 2016), and the involvement of Korea Trade Insurance Corporation in Gaziantep reflected a recent strategy by the South Korean government to use the agency to support the Korea Development Bank's investments in what were considered higher-risk settings (Businesskorea, 2014). In total, the South Korean government provided or guaranteed around half of the total loans used to finance the Gaziantep health campus.

The awarding of the Gaziantep health campus project came amidst a wider push by the South Korean government to promote healthcare export opportunities across much of Asia, including through high-level events and trade discussions supplemented by the offer of financing from public and private agencies in South Korea. In 2015, South Korea and Iran held a bilateral conference aimed at fostering trade and investment between the countries, and six months later Hyundai and Samsung had signed agreements with the Iranian government to develop public hospitals in Shiraz, Tehran and Mazandaran, financed by loans from the Export-Import Bank of Korea (Financial Tribune, 2015, 2016; Hayes, 2016). Countries falling within the bounds of North Korea's 'New Northern' policy, which since 2017 aims to foster economic and political relations with select Asian countries at a more northerly latitude to South Korea, have proved a particular focus for recent activities. Samsung has secured a series of Export-Import Bank of Korea–funded contracts in Mongolia (Samsung C&T, 2019), while Turkmenistan, Uzbekistan and Kazakhstan have been targeted for developments of this kind (Ministry of Health and Welfare, 2019). Long-term construction and management contracts of the kind used in Gaziantep and Turkey's other health campuses can be particularly lucrative, and in 2018 the South Korean government created a state-owned company called Korea Overseas Infrastructure & Urban Development Corporation to work with other governments on identifying opportunities for public-private partnership projects across several sectors, including healthcare. The first success appears to be in Kazakhstan, where Korea Overseas Infrastructure & Urban Development Corporation recently signed an agreement with the Kazakhstan government to collaborate on the financing and construction of hospitals and roads using public-private partnership models (Baiterek, 2019).

One key group of beneficiaries from all these projects are the South Korean companies like Samsung and Hyundai that obtain contracts. They belong to a group of companies known as 'chaebols' – family-run industrial conglomerates that have historically been highly favoured and heavily supported by South Korea's developmental state as part of a 'state-banks-chaebols nexus' (Shin & Chang, 2003, p. 4) – they are archetypical national champions. Although their close ties to the South Korean government were challenged to some extent by governance reforms following the 1997 Asian Financial Crisis, they persist through formal and informal arrangements (You, 2021). Samsung's website emphasises its ability to broker financing deals from the South Korean government in the form of concessional (ODA-eligible) loans and export credits, noting, 'we maintain a close relationship with Korean Export Credit Agencies, such as K-EXIM [Export-Import Bank of Korea] and K-SURE [Korea Trade Insurance Corporation] for a long time to help the governmental clients to finance the infrastructure projects' (Samsung C&T, 2022).

But potential benefits for the South Korean state extend beyond support for a national champion in global healthcare markets. The South Korean government itself stands to benefit financially from projects where loans are returnable and accompanied by generous interest payments. Investors in the Gaziantep project are reported to expect 7–9 per cent returns on their investments (Cho, 2014). Such is the attraction of the debt and its repayments that in 2017 KIAMCO created a new investment fund and used it to acquire USD 63 million in debt owed to investors for another of Turkey's health campuses, in Mersin (Pulse, 2017). The debt was insured against political risks by global insurer AON and the World Bank's Multilateral Investment Guarantee Agency, a measure reflecting concerns after the attempted coup in Turkey in 2016, and returns were expected to be in the region of 8–9 per cent (D. Kim, 2018). According to one anonymous source reported in the business media, the new fund was seen by KIAMCO as a 'springboard for domestic investors', in particular insurance companies, looking to deepen their involvement in Turkey's health campus projects (Kim, 2018). In seeking to use state investments overseas to benefit the financial services industry (rather than necessarily infrastructure and technology companies), the move aligned South Korea with states such as the Netherlands that are pursuing similar ambitions through the healthcare sector.

7 Singapore, Malaysia and Sovereign Wealth Funds

In this final pair of case studies, I outline one of the most striking and yet poorly documented developments in the ownership of healthcare: how two states – Singapore and Malaysia – emerged as key shareholders in the infrastructure serving the health needs of Asia's growing middle-class populations. In these cases, it has been sovereign wealth funds which provide the mechanism for state investment; agencies of the state driven by a financial mission to protect and augment national wealth. Their entry into overseas healthcare systems has taken place in parallel to the work of DFIs and national development banks, but they now form part of the same financialised regime for corporate investment and expansion in healthcare.

Singapore

The 1997 Asian Financial Crisis was an opportunity for the Singapore government, which had emerged relatively unscathed by the crisis, to double-down on plans for the country to become a hub for global investment into, and out of, Asia (Monetary Authority of Singapore, 1998). Alongside a series of regulatory reforms, the government began to adjust how it used its sovereign wealth funds – GIC and Temasek – in order to meet this ambition. GIC was instructed to place greater emphasis on achieving larger returns for its funds, rather than simply maintaining its value as a national 'contingency fund', and so was given flexibility to make longer-term, riskier investments in Asia's 'emerging markets' (GIC, 2013). It was also directed to operate more of its funds through Singapore-based investment management companies, providing a boost to those companies and the local financial services industry. Temasek, which had historically managed government stakes in Singapore's strategic industries, such as transport and communications, was also to begin expanding its geographical remit to encompass a wider 'Asian presence' (Temasek, 2005, p. 27). The vision for Singapore's sovereign wealth funds would open up new sectors to their investment, eventually taking them into the healthcare systems of neighbouring countries where there were opportunities for investment in rapidly growing corporate hospital chains.

In 2003, GIC made its first investment in an overseas healthcare provider – Australia's largest private hospital operator Mayne. Mayne was in dire straits financially and had reported annual losses of USD 300 million that year, but it owned three hospitals in Indonesia and was well placed to expand into Asia's healthcare markets, making it a valuable prospect to investors eyeing growth potential. GIC joined a consortium led by a subsidiary of Citigroup (itself one of the largest investors in the US private healthcare system) and Australia-based investment fund Ironbridge Capital, to acquire Mayne for USD 560 million (CNN, 2003; Wynne, 2004). They re-branded the provider as Affinity Health, separated its hospitals from its pharmaceutical arm and drew up plans to develop a chain of hospitals spanning Indonesia, Malaysia, India and China

(Greenblat, 2005). Those ambitious plans never came to fruition, however, as the consortium soon sold Affinity to rival Australian provider Ramsay in 2005 in a deal that proved too enticing to turn down: the consortium reportedly made a staggering combined *profit* of more than USD 450 million (Evans, 2005). In a sector where financially driven sovereign wealth funds had previously shown little interest, the deal demonstrated the scale of returns that were possible.

Temasek's entry into overseas healthcare markets came soon after GIC but was somewhat more tentative. First, in 2004, the company made a USD 11 million investment in renowned Indian healthcare provider Apollo, taking a small stake in the company in the process (Temasek, 2005). Temasek had earmarked India as a key target for its investments and saw service sectors such as healthcare as an attractive proposition for growth given India's relatively cheap labour costs (p. 27). Apollo was a prime target: a well-established chain of hospitals in South Asia which needed to refinance debts incurred by its rapid growth (Rediff.com, 2004). Temasek even followed up with an investment (alongside JP Morgan) in Apollo's healthcare consultancy spin-off Apollo Health Street (Temasek, 2005). Soon after, Temasek made its second commitment to an overseas healthcare provider: investing USD 27.5 million in Thailand's Bumrungrad Hospital (The Star, 2006), on the basis of its 'good domestic and regional growth potential' (Temasek, 2006). Bumrungrad is famed for its status as a global hub for healthcare travellers and has been referred to by some as 'The Mecca of Medical Tourism' (Aron, 2009). The hospital had ambitious plans to expand within Asia and had already entered into management contracts with facilities in Yangon and Dhaka (Arunanondchai & Fink, 2006), taken a majority stake in Asian Hospital after the Manila facility's IFC-led restructuring (IFC, 2008a) and announced plans to build a hospital in Dubai in collaboration with the Dubai government's investment company Istithmar (Al Bawaba, 2006). Temasek's investment in Bumrungrad was made in collaboration with Istithmar, bringing the states of Dubai and Singapore together as co-investors in one of Thailand's leading hospitals.

The Global Financial Crisis unfolding after 2007 was accompanied by a short hiatus in healthcare investments for Singapore's sovereign wealth funds, but they soon ratcheted up activity again. Temasek was first, focusing its interest in India's corporate healthcare sector, where a small number of chains were engaged in a frenzied expansion for market share in the country's urban areas. Over the 2010s Temasek's investments in India included: USD 27 million in hospital provider and insurer Max Healthcare (Singh, 2010); USD 26 million for oncology chain Healthcare Global (Reuters, 2013); USD 100 million for Medanta hospitals (J. Johnson, 2015); USD 153 million for Manipal hospitals (Kurian, 2017), and USD 38 million for eye care chain Dr Agarwal's Healthcare

(Chandrashekhar, 2019). This was approximately double the total investments made by CDC Group in India's private healthcare provision during the same period (USD 181 million – see Section 4). Temasek also started to make inroads into other large healthcare markets in Asia, investing USD 250 million into a joint venture with USA-based Colombia Pacific that aimed to develop a chain of healthcare facilities across China (Business Wire, 2016). Such was the rapid growth and ambition of its healthcare investments that in 2014 Temasek set up a subsidiary company – Sheares Healthcare – dedicated to organising and managing its burgeoning portfolio of healthcare investments.

GIC took a wider, regional approach spanning several countries. It had a tumultuous experience in India with eye care chain Vasan: an initial investment of USD 100 million in 2012 was followed by another USD 20 million two years later, to attempt to restructure debts, but the company entered a downward spiral of losses, investigations over unpaid taxes and allegations of money laundering and faced insolvency (Shukla, 2016), resulting in its acquisition by rival chain ASG (Pilla, 2022). GIC's focus has instead shifted to Southeast Asia. In 2014, it invested USD 84 million in Philippines hospital chain Metro Pacific, and in 2019 joined a consortium that collectively invested another USD 580 million in the chain to help fund ambitious plans to more than double its number of hospitals (from 14 to 30) in the country within ten years (GIC, 2014, 2019). These investments were followed by GIC leading its own consortium to invest USD 200 million in Vietnam's Vinmec chain to support its domestic growth (Reuters, 2020), and in 2021 it invested USD 180 million in Malaysia's Sunway (GIC, 2021). Regarding the latter investment, GIC's Head of Direct Investments for Southeast Asia noted the provider's growth potential in the context of Malaysia's ageing but increasingly affluent and insured domestic population, and the likely resumption of medical tourism to Malaysia after COVID-related travel restrictions ease (GIC, 2021).

The rationale for these healthcare investments by Singapore's sovereign wealth funds has been bluntly financial, with little, if any, reference to other considerations. Organisational materials refer to investments being made because of the potential for growth amongst providers who can serve the healthcare needs of domestic middle-class populations and/or those of medical tourists from within and outside the region. Indeed, many of the countries where investments have been made, such as Thailand, India and Malaysia, already have substantial provision infrastructure, with much of it aimed at global medical tourism markets. While growth in size remains a focal point for the funds' activities, other strategies for value creation are being adopted too, as indicated by Temasek's healthcare-focused subsidiary Sheares, which describes its work in terms of improving the business models of its providers, encouraging innovation and 'shaping the future of healthcare delivery with a focus on Asia' (Sheares, 2022). For that vision statement to come from a state-owned entity is testament to the scale and ambition of investor states in healthcare, something mirrored by the recent history of Malaysia's interests in this sector.

Malaysia

On 25 November 2005, a member of Malaysia's ruling party stood in Parliament and, to the applause of colleagues, criticised the growing role of Singaporean and US investors in Malaysia's healthcare system (Parlimen Malaysia, 2005). The comments were part of a debate on the performance of government healthcare contracts, and the failures of Malaysia-based provider Pantai – a company immersed in the politics and cronyism of turn-of-the-century Malaysia and described in Chee's (2008) examination of financial capital interests in Malaysia's healthcare system as a 'prime example of rentier capital in healthcare' (p. 2150). The company had been part-owned by the Malaysian Prime Minister's son Mokhzani Mahathir and benefitted from large government contracts for medical examination and licensing. But in 2001, amid growing criticism of cronyism and continued economic repercussions of the Asian Financial Crisis, Mahathir sold his stake in Pantai to a Malaysian businessman (Reuters, 2001), and within a few years the businessman sold that stake on to Singapore-based hospital chain Parkway – a company created by two Malaysian property developers living in Singapore which by 2005 had a network of hospitals within Singapore, Malaysia and Indonesia (Jayaseelan, 2010; Wynne, 2000).

Parkway became Pantai's largest shareholder when it acquired its 30 per cent stake in Pantai in 2005, creating a problem for Malaysia's government. The change saw the inducements of Pantai's large government contracts, seen as serving the patronage of domestic 'Bumiputera' ethnic groups, instead being diverted to stakeholders based overseas. But it also weakened the Malaysian government's influence over its own industrial strategy for healthcare, a sector that had been earmarked as key for Malaysia's economic development (Chee, 2010). In the aftermath of the Asian Financial Crisis, which had affected Malaysia severely, the export of healthcare services (primarily in the form of cross-border travel for healthcare) offered a way to capitalise on Malaysia's advanced healthcare system and bring much-needed foreign currency into the country. Pantai and Parkway, together the largest group of private healthcare providers in Malaysia, were going to be key to achieving this strategy.

The government responded quickly to Parkway's part-acquisition of Pantai by taking ownership of the latter using its sovereign wealth fund Khazanah

Nasional. The Malaysian government had already set out a post-Asian Financial Crisis growth strategy for Khazanah that involved entering new sectors and making more investments overseas (Khazanah Nasional Berhad, 2021), and this new approach had led Khazanah into its first healthcare investment – USD 44 million in India's Apollo Hospitals (Khazanah Nasional Berhad, 2005). The Pantai predicament represented an opportunity to maintain this new strategy while protecting the domestic political interests of the government. Khazanah soon announced a complex arrangement that saw Khazanah take a small share of Parkway and majority ownership of Pantai, while Parkway's stake in Pantai would be limited to 40 per cent. There was explicit acknowledgement of the Malaysian interests being served by the deal, as well as the potential for private healthcare growth:

> Both Khazanah and Parkway are committed to comply with all Malaysian regulations and policies in relation to Pantai's concession assets, including in respect of the requirements for Bumiputera ownership and Bumiputera representation. We believe the strategic interests of the nation will be protected in this manner and the commercial interests of Pantai and its investors – including both major and minority investors – will also be served with this partnership. We also believe the proposed partnership with its linkages to leading regional and international players in this field will accelerate the development of private healthcare in Malaysia with the benefits ultimately flowing to the Malaysian public in terms of better services at competitive prices. (Khazanah Nasional Berhad, 2006)

The resolution lasted just a few years, however, as the issue again came to a head in 2010 when one of Parkway's other investors, TPG, sold its 24 per cent stake in Parkway to the owners of Indian hospital chain Fortis for USD 685 million (Sapkala, 2010). Khazanah had reportedly been offered TPG's shares but declined to bid for them given the short notice provided of just three days (Gabriel, 2010). For Fortis, its involvement in Parkway was part of an ambitious programme for expansion that had included recent purchases of Indian rival Wockhardt's hospitals, and construction of a hospital in Mauritius (Lefebvre, 2010). However, the company's arrival on the board of Parkway disrupted Khazanah's influence. Not only was Fortis now the largest single shareholder in the healthcare provider, but it also took majority control of Parkway's board of thirteen by augmenting its own four director positions with agreements for three other board members to vote with them (K. Brown, 2010). Within months, as board relations soured over management and governance within Parkway, Khazanah developed an offer to Parkway's shareholders that would see Khazanah attempt to buy shares totalling 51.5 per cent of the company (K. Brown, 2010). Fortis quickly responded with a counter-offer to itself become majority shareholder, leading to a showdown: on one side, the Malaysian government and its Khazanah sovereign wealth fund; on the other, Indian chain Fortis, a suite of Indian banks (including several owned by the Indian government) lined up to loan Fortis funds for the takeover (The Economic Times, 2010), and Singapore's GIC, which was planning a USD 82 million investment in Fortis (Hindustan Times, 2010; Singh & Chatterjee, 2011). The involvement of India, Malaysia and Singapore – three key hubs for healthcare travel in the region – led to one commentator describing the wrestle for control as 'Asia's biggest play on medical tourism' (Financial Times, 2010).

In the end, Fortis relented and Khazanah won out. Reports at the time indicated that a factor in Fortis' withdrawal from the process was the Singaporean government's reluctance to go head-to-head with the Malaysian government at a time of thawing relations and recently signed land and development deals (Choudhary & Lim, 2010). Khazanah used a recently formed subsidiary – Integrated Healthcare Holdings (IHH) – to acquire Parkway for USD 2.6 billion (Khazanah Nasional, 2010; Venkat et al., 2010), leaving the Malaysian government, through Khazanah and IHH, in control of swathes of private healthcare provision infrastructure spanning Singapore, Malaysia, Indonesia, India, China, Brunei and Vietnam. The following year IHH then added Acibadem's hospitals in Turkey and North Macedonia to its burgeoning portfolio (Mitsui, 2011).

Domestic politics have since diluted Khazanah's role in IHH. In 2012 Khazanah launched an initial public offering (IPO) for IHH, as part of a Malaysian government strategy to divest from specific sectors and encourage private investment. The IPO valued the company at a colossal USD 8 billion (Ngui & Kok, 2012), and still left Khazanah with 47 per cent of IHH shares (Grant, 2012). It also presented new opportunities for patronage: the listing in Malaysia was managed by CIMB, a state-owned bank run by the Prime Minister's brother, and offered 2 per cent of the shares to the Malaysian public via a ballot (IHH Healthcare Berhad, 2012), while a sizeable portion of shares (8 per cent) was bought by Malaysian public pension provider Employees Provident Fund Board. Then in 2018, in the aftermath of an election that saw the first change in ruling party in Malaysia's history, the new government declared healthcare as 'non-core' business for Khazanah and sold a tranche of IHH shares to Japanese sogo shosha Mitsui (see Section 6) (L. Lee & Daga, 2018). Khazanah remains the second largest shareholder in IHH, and occupies the position of Chair on the board, though it has been rumoured to be considering selling its remaining stake to Mitsui (The Star, 2021).

The growing influence of sovereign wealth funds in Asia's healthcare systems is perhaps best illustrated by the way in which Malaysia Khazanah (through IHH) and Singapore's Temasek have competed for control of India's corporate hospital chains. In 2015, IHH and Temasek were each reported to be interested in buying into India's CARE Hospitals, though in the end it was private equity fund Abraaj and UK DFI CDC Group that succeeded (Advent International, 2016). IHH opted to instead buy majority stakes in two other Indian chains – Continental Hospitals and Global Hospitals (Balakrishnan & Indulal PM., 2019) – irking Apollo founder Pratap Reddy who objected to IHH investing in Apollo's rivals (Khazanah sold its Apollo shares not long afterwards – Economic Times, 2017). In 2018, Temasek and IHH were in separate discussions to buy majority stakes in Delhi's Medanta Medicity hospital, though neither ultimately progressed to completion (Balakrishnan & PM, 2019; Sonavane, 2021). Later that same year, in a remarkable turn of events from the 'Asia's biggest play on medical tourism' standoff of eight years prior, IHH had an offer accepted to take control of the Fortis chain of hospitals in a deal worth up to USD 1.1 billion (Altstedter, 2018). In doing so IHH outbid several rival consortia, including one led by Manipal hospitals (in which Temasek had invested USD 153 million just one year prior). After failing to acquire Fortis, Temasek-backed Manipal instead committed USD 241 million to purchase the India hospitals of Columbia Asia, which IHH had also been rumoured to have considered buying (Mint, 2020). This decade-long process of negotiation, acquisition and consolidation has seen Temasek-backed Manipal and Khazanah-backed IHH emerge as, respectively, the second and third largest private providers in the country, behind Apollo (Ghosh, 2021).

8 Conclusions

In this Elements volume I have used an investor state lens – a perspective that studies the institutions, activities and justifications through which states engage *as*, *with* and *for* investors in other countries – to examine how states are becoming key financial stakeholders in the healthcare systems of other countries. This perspective combines analysis of specific investments with an understanding of the broader institutional context behind such investments. It pays particular attention to the alliances of public and private organisations that come together to make (co-)investments, shedding light on how the institutional landscape of global health is evolving in the Sustainable Development Goal era.

In applying the investor state lens to a series of cases, I have shown how a range of states and state financing institutions are fuelling the rapid expansion of particular models of (usually corporate-oriented) healthcare projects regionally and globally (Table 4). This has included examples of European states using DFIs (Sections 4 and 5), and Asian states using national development banks and

Table 4 Summary of cases

State	Financing institution(s) and instruments primarily involved	Geographic foci for investments	Models of healthcare provision	Typical justification(s) for healthcare investments
UK	BII (DFI); equity investments	Middle-income countries globally, but particularly in Anglophone Africa and Asia	Private hospitals/clinics	Development
France	Proparco (DFI); equity investments and loans	Middle-income countries globally, but particularly in North Africa and the Middle East	Private hospitals/clinics and public-private partnerships	Development
Sweden	Swedfund (DFI); equity investments and loans	Select middle-income countries globally	Private hospitals/clinics	Development and business interests
Netherlands	FMO (DFI); equity investments and grants	Select middle-income countries in Africa and Asia	Private hospitals/clinics	Development and business interests

Japan	JBIC (national development bank); loans and guarantees	Middle-income and high-income countries in Asia and Europe	Private hospitals/clinics and public-private partnerships	Business interests
South Korea	Korea Development Bank (national development bank); loans and guarantees	Middle-income countries in Asia and Europe	Public-private partnerships	Business interests
Singapore	GIC and Temasek (sovereign wealth fund); equity investments	Middle-income and high-income countries in Asia	Private hospitals/clinics	Financial motivations
Malaysia	Khazanah Nasional (sovereign wealth fund); equity investments	Middle-income countries in Asia and Europe	Private hospitals/clinics	Financial motivations

sovereign wealth funds (Sections 6 and 7). The growth trajectories shown for these cases indicate that this is a trend which emerged in the past 20–25 years, and which has been gathering pace in the past 10–15 years. It is a trend being driven by the end of aid, in which many states are graduating from aid-recipient status and engaging in development financing on their own terms, while OECD states look to the reciprocal benefits of a wider package of development financing beyond aid. These changes are encouraging new forms of state activity in which healthcare systems are being positioned as zones for corporate expansion and financial accumulation.

In the cases of the UK and France, their national DFIs have built a portfolio of healthcare investments across continents, often working through intermediary fund managers or in tandem with private investors. These two states have historically been prominent participants in the OECD donor community, and key contributors of ODA to the states of their former empires, and in a global policy context that is shifting away from the donor-recipient relations of aid they appear to be pursuing broadly similar colonial geographies for their DFI investments. They have been amongst the most enthusiastic advocates of the potential development benefits of state and non-state investments in private healthcare projects, with less emphasis placed on securing domestic economic gains than other states. However, in recent years they have drifted towards a more overt pursuit of national interests in development financing, using DFIs to secure large infrastructure contracts for domestic business (France) and giving greater regard to the potential benefits for a domestic financial services industry (UK).

Sweden and the Netherlands have a stronger history of using DFIs to promote the interests of domestic business. They have sought to bolster the expansion of national champion companies in overseas contexts using joint ventures and loan guarantees to co-invest and reduce risks; or grants that subsidise the trialling of new healthcare models. Their healthcare investments have been relatively small and targeted, but in both cases health has recently been identified as a priority area for investment. This is justified ostensibly on development grounds but also offers substantial commercial benefits to Swedish and Dutch healthcare industries; in the case of the Netherlands, there are benefits for the Dutch financial services industries too. Though Sweden has downplayed the relationship between its DFI and domestic interests in recent years, the Netherlands has moved in the opposite direction – intensifying its efforts to use development financing to pursue a domestic business agenda.

The cases of Japan and South Korea share some similarities with Sweden and Netherlands. Investments in healthcare have been targeted with the explicit intention of supporting the global expansion of national champion conglomerates and, in the case of South Korea, a financial services industry. In both cases there is a longer history of exporting health products and catering to medical tourism markets, and this has provided the foundations for a strategic move into overseas markets for healthcare infrastructure, particularly within the rapidly expanding healthcare systems of Asia. The concerted advocacy efforts and scale of state resources being deployed is indicative of the short- and longer-term value of infrastructure projects that have generous returns for investors and that will serve as demonstrations when national champion companies pitch for overseas contracts in future.

In the cases of Singapore and Malaysia, investments have seen these states emerge as owners of foreign healthcare companies with national and continental reach. Their sovereign wealth funds, originally tasked with augmenting national wealth, have taken on wider remits to protect and promote industries of national strategic interest (including financial services in the case of Singapore, and healthcare in the case of Malaysia). Healthcare has become a sector where such strategic interests can be pursued while still meeting core institutional principles of preserving and enhancing national wealth. These states have made investments on a scale that has tended to far exceed that of the other states discussed in this volume, focusing their attention on Asia's rapidly growing healthcare systems and the corporate providers now consolidating positions within them.

Investor States in a Financialised Regime for Global Health

The cases show how eight different states have engaged as investors in healthcare systems in ways that are rarely addressed within scholarship on global health financing and governance. That scholarship has tended to focus on the institutions and relations of aid, which is understandable given the significant influence of aid relations, past and present. However, as the global development policy context continues to move from development *aid* to development *financing* (Mawdsley & Taggart, 2022), there is a need to devote more analytical attention to the wider systems of development financing now being directed to health-related issues, including the returnable investments made by state and non-state actors.

One area for closer examination, as demonstrated by this Elements volume, is the states and institutions involved. The cases of European states examined, and their use of DFIs, show how 'beyond aid' trends in global health are retaining some of the relations of aid. These include a positioning of states such as the UK and France at the forefront of developments, adopting similar language and visions of development as used in aid, and in some cases overlapping colonial geographies. The interest in mutual benefit evident amongst the European states is long-standing in aid relations, and the pursuit by some states of benefits for national champion companies is not new either – many governments have placed formal or informal restrictions on their aid transfers in order to subsidise domestic industries through a practice known as 'tied aid' (Clay et al., 2009) and in some cases have even stipulated a portion of aid that should remain within the sending country; in Denmark this has been openly acknowledged as the 'return percentage' (Selbervik & Nygaard, 2006). But the institutions involved in these processes (DFIs) and the instruments involved (such as equity investments and private sector loans) are largely new to global health, as is the more overt emphasis on securing (usually economic) returns, including the return to investors of financing, with interest or value added. In examining these activities and motivations, and tracing their evolution over time, the volume consolidates and deepens a small, but growing, body of literature that has sought to track and scrutinise the investments being made by DFIs in healthcare systems and their implications for equitable access to healthcare (Hamer & Kapilashrami, 2020; Hunter & Marriott, 2018; Hunter & Murray, 2015; Wemos, 2020). The volume shows how, in the policy context of the end of aid, a set of states are using DFIs, private healthcare projects and the language of development as cover for pursuing domestic interests in the global health arena.

The cases of Asian states included in this Element highlight the activities being performed, often in parallel to those of DFIs, by sets of institutions (and indeed states) that have been largely overlooked in the study of global health (see journal special section by Tan et al., 2012, for reviews of the aid and global health diplomacy of Asian states). While Japan and South Korea have been recognised to some extent in global health as providers of aid, their use of national development banks and export credit agencies to pursue overseas public-private partnership contracts and benefit domestic industries in health-care has escaped scrutiny. Singapore and Malaysia are acknowledged even less as participants in global health, and yet this volume shows how extensive their regional involvement as healthcare investors has been over the past twenty years. The activities of these states appear, on the whole, to have less to do with ideas of global health and development, and more to do with national economic strategies, histories of developmental state intervention in economic activity, and a contemporary phase of state capitalism characterised by transnationalisation. The strong focus of these states on investing within the Asian continent reflects the strong growth potential of healthcare systems in the region, and the financial benefits on offer to foreign contractors and investors, but in the cases of Japan and South Korea may also be a response to the growth of Chinese investments regionally and the perceived influence this confers. It is a trend that positions these states as prominent, if under-acknowledged, actors in the evolving institutional landscape for global health.

More than a decade ago, amidst the growing influence of a securitisation agenda within global health, Lakoff (2010) elaborated what might be considered two 'regimes' of actors and interests existing simultaneous within global health – global health security and humanitarian biomedicine. The findings of this Elements volume contribute to growing understanding of a contemporary regime for global health that might be termed 'financialised'. As I and others have shown (Busfield, 2020; Hughes-McLure & Mawdsley, 2022; Hunter & Murray, 2019; Sell & Williams, 2020; Stein, 2021; Stein & Sridhar, 2018), global health is becoming subject to the deepening penetration of a set of financial motives, markets, actors and institutions. An investor state perspective shows the contributions of states within this financialised regime, the role of financial institutions such as DFIs, national development banks and sovereign wealth funds, and of notions of returns on investment.

The Elements volume also sheds light on the interactions between different actors in the emerging financialised regime for global health, including the relationships being built between investor states and with multilateral and non-state investors. I have highlighted instances where European DFIs co-invested in intermediary fund managers and healthcare projects alongside other national DFIs, the IFC, regional development banks, philanthropic foundations, multinational corporations and private equity funds; and where national development banks from Japan and South Korea invested alongside suites of private banks. These kinds of interactions are being encouraged by leading actors such as the IFC and through initiatives like the Investors for Health network which use the sustainable development financing gap as justification for expanded roles for private finance in global health. But while attempts to fuse the language and operations of development and finance may go some way to promoting collaborative working between these different groups of actors, there is also potential for divergence and disagreement when operating in a highly competitive commercial environment. I have shown instances where investor states bump together in the hunt for business opportunities and financial returns, and where the relationship between investor state and investee breaks down. The Abraaj scandal remains a stark reminder of the risks of aligning global health with a financial services industry better known for grotesque acts of consumption and wealth accumulation.[11]

---

[11] Among the many revelations of the Abraaj scandal and the insights it provided into the workings of state and private finance was a claim that Naqvi himself considered 'partnership capital' a ruse to attract investment from development organisations and that it 'shouldn't be taken seriously' as a concept (S. Clark & Louch, 2021, p. 106).

Where Equities Diverge

The ascent of investor states in global health has required and produced institutional models for healthcare provision in which investments can be readily made and returned, and this has long-term implications for equitable access to healthcare. One form used is that of the 'public-private partnership' financing model for hospital construction, in which a private consortium builds the healthcare infrastructure using financing from external sources and then is repaid by the commissioning government over subsequent years and decades. The model has received considerable support from a range of governments, multilateral organisations and consultancies who argue that it provides a useful mechanism for governments to raise capital quickly (World Bank, 2013b). But it has also been criticised for its relatively high costs to commissioning governments compared to other forms of public financing and the knock-on effects for health budgets (Eurodad, 2018), and there are examples of spiralling costs for commissioning governments and prohibitive bills for early repayment (D. Campbell, 2019; Oxfam, 2014).

In Sections 4 and 6 I showed how three investor states – France, Japan and South Korea – have financed public-private partnership projects in Turkey by providing loans or guarantees totalling USD 2 billion. Their investments ensured that national champion companies could secure the large infrastructure contracts involved, and South Korea at least is engaged in a wider campaign to promote this model for hospital construction to governments in Asia, with some recent success in Kazakhstan. In Turkey the public-private partnership model appears to prioritise political patronage in the form of new hospitals that will be popular with the electorate, and large contracts for favoured Turkish construction companies. But the substantial long-term costs facing the Turkish state are now becoming apparent as project costs have risen due to devaluation of the Turkish lira, and expensive state repayment schedules have commenced. The leader of Turkey's main opposition party has accused the Turkish government of systematically 'robbing the state' through its health campus initiative (Sonmez, 2021), raising questions about the appropriateness of DFI and national development bank support for the model.

The second institutional form is that of the corporate healthcare provider. This is a model for healthcare provision which has been growing rapidly (Lethbridge, 2015), and which sees chains of providers emerging across middle-income countries such as China (Baru and Nundy, 2020), India (Kapilashrami & Baru, 2018; Lefebvre, 2010) and Turkey (Eren Vural, 2017). State and non-state loans and equity investments have fuelled the expansion of these providers through greenfield development and the acquisition of other providers, and throughout the volume I have drawn attention to these kinds of activities by investor states. It has been most pronounced with the cases involving DFIs and sovereign wealth funds, fuelling the expansion of private healthcare chains in middle-income countries across the world. India has been a particular focal point for states such as the UK, Singapore and Malaysia, reflecting the relative maturity of its corporate health-care sector and the substantial opportunities for growth in a context of under-resourced public healthcare provision and its status as a medical tourism destination.

The kind of private for-profit healthcare provision being expanded by investor states requires users to pay fees out-of-pocket, or through private or social health insurance. This has three key implications for healthcare access. First, it excludes and marginalises people who struggle to afford fees unless public subsidies can be obtained in the form of social health insurance pro-grammes. Second, it encourages segmentation within healthcare systems such that wealthy (domestic and global) users can access a superior level of corpor-ate-provided services while the remainder of the population is reliant on whatever public services remain available in the face of competition with the corporate private sector for finite resources such as health workers (Hunter & Murray, 2019). Third, it entrenches commercial motivations which are particu-larly problematic in a sector that governs life and death; as I have documented with others, private healthcare in India is now steeped in investment and management practices designed to extract wealth (Marathe et al., 2020), and which largely defy effective state regulation (Hunter et al., 2022). These problems are likely to manifest in a growing range of settings as state and non-state investors fuel the national and regional expansion of private for-profit healthcare chains.

The dominance of private for-profit healthcare provision as asset class within investor state activities sees one interpretation of 'equity' being subordinated to another. On the one hand, *equity as fairness*: where healthcare is provided on the basis of need, according to principles of universality, and healthcare organisations are accountable to the populations they serve. On the other, *equity as financial capital*: where healthcare is provided on the basis of ability to pay; according to principles of profit and value creation, and healthcare organisations are account-able to their investors. Some commentators have claimed that these kinds of divergent perspectives can be brought together through the language and public subsidies of universal health coverage (Krech et al., 2018; Wadge et al., 2017b), and I have shown in earlier sections how investor states have engaged with these ideas to varying degrees. However, there is a rapidly growing body of work questioning that narrative and the limited entitlements and redistribution that its model for 'universal health coverage' entails (Hamer & Kapilashrami, 2020;

Jubilee Debt Campaign, 2017; Lethbridge, 2016; Marriott & Hamer, 2014; Wemos, 2020). In the cases examined in this volume, equitable access to healthcare has been at best a minor consideration for investor states and their financing institutions, and far less of a concern than the pursuit of political and economic benefits. There is a need and opportunity for civil society actors to (continue to) press state-owned financing institutions for greater attention to issues of equitable access in their investment decision-making processes.

Opportunities for Research

The trends I have outlined in this volume have largely escaped the attention of a global health field that has tended to instead focus on the impacts and governance of development aid. This is understandable given the scale and influence of aid relations in global health which continue to outweigh the kinds of transfers examined in this volume. However, the context of the end of aid, the broader set of financing arrangements it engenders and the range of states taking this path necessitate closer examination within the broader context of the global political economy for health and development (Alami, Dixon, & Mawdsley, 2021; Sell & Williams, 2020). Below I identify four areas for future study.

First, there is an opportunity for contextually grounded research that examines the policy processes that open up healthcare systems in specific locations to foreign investment. Governments may be active to greater or lesser degrees in enabling and encouraging foreign investment into healthcare systems, and it will be important to understand the processes and rationale for liberalising healthcare provision in these ways, the lobbying involved and issues of state capture, and how it interplays with the impacts of the COVID-19 pandemic. Researchers can pay particular attention to if and how the involvement of foreign states complicates notions of sovereignty in these policy-making processes.

Second, detailed research on the working practices and relations that exist within state financing institutions could offer insights into how the sector operates and the ambitions and practices involved. A 'peopled' approach to the study of investor states could shed light on the individual and networked relationships that develop between state and non-state institutions, the process of selecting targets for investment and non-state co-investors, and the evolution and diffusion of ideas and practices within and between institutions. Such research could also illuminate understanding of the boardroom interactions that take place within healthcare companies and which are liable to shape the future of healthcare provision in many settings.

Third, better understanding of the zones and apparatus for regulating and governing investor state activities could inform advocacy for the equitable use of resources. Building on the above, this could include the formal and informal rules that influence how financing institutions operate, where they invest and how. It could also point to the institutional, national and international regulations that shape their working, and the potential for future intervention in these regulatory domains.

Fourth, the impacts of the investments on equitable access to healthcare. Given current trends, the preferred asset classes of foreign investors are likely to become dominant models for healthcare provision in many countries in the coming decades. To date, researchers have relied on inference using the business models of invested companies (Hamer & Kapilashrami, 2020; Wemos, 2020). There is a pressing need for research which can rigorously identify access and resourcing issues that are already emerging now, to feed into public policy processes in a range of contexts.

Acronyms and Abbreviations

BII	British International Investment
COVID-19	Coronavirus disease
DEG	Deutsche Investitions und Entwicklungsgesellschaft
DFI	Development finance institution
EUR	European Union Euro
FMO	Financierings-Maatschappij voor Ontwikkelingslanden
GIC	Government of Singapore Investment Corporation
IFC	International Finance Corporation
IHH	Integrated Healthcare Holdings
IHME	Institute for Health Metrics and Evaluation
IPO	Initial public offering
JBIC	Japan Bank for International Cooperation
JICA	Japan International Cooperation Agency
KIAMCO	Korea Development Bank Infrastructure Investments Asset Management Company
ODA	Official development assistance
OECD	Organisation for Economic Cooperation and Development
SDG	Sustainable Development Goal
TOSSD	Total official support for sustainable development
UK	United Kingdom
UNCTAD	United Nations Conference on Trade and Development
USA	United States of America
USD	USA dollar

References

Abrar, P. (2011). *Vaatsalya healthcare raises $10mn in third round of PE funding*. The Economic Times. https://economictimes.indiatimes.com/indus try/healthcare/biotech/healthcare/vaatsalya-healthcare-raises-10-mn-in-third-round-of-pe-funding/articleshow/8831407.cms?from=mdr.

Advent International. (2016, January 13). *The Abraaj Group agrees to acquire a majority stake in CARE Hospitals, a leading healthcare provider in India, from Advent International*. www.adventinternational.com/the-abraaj-group-agrees-to-acquire-a-majority-stake-in-care-hospitals-a-leading-healthcare-provider-in-india-from-advent-international/.

African Medical and Research Foundation. (2022). *Partnership for primary care: A sustainable model to revolutionize primary care*. https://amref.org/partnershipforprimarycare/.

Al Bawaba. (2006, January 31). *Istithmar, Bumrungrad International sign JV for new hospital in Dubai*. www.albawaba.com/business/istithmar-bumrun-grad-international-sign-jv-new-hospital-dubai.

Alami, I., Babic, M., Dixon, A. D., & Liu, I. T. (2022). Special issue introduction: What is the new state capitalism? *Contemporary Politics*, 1–19, 245–63. https://doi.org/10.1080/13569775.2021.2022336.

Alami, I., & Dixon, A. D. (2020a). State capitalism(s) redux? Theories, tensions, controversies. *Competition & Change*, *24*(1), 70–94. https://doi.org/10.1177/1024529419881949.

Alami, I., & Dixon, A. D. (2020b). The strange geographies of the 'new' state capitalism. *Political Geography*, *82*, 102237. https://doi.org/10.1016/j.polgeo.2020.102237.

Alami, I., & Dixon, A. D. (2021). Uneven and combined state capitalism. *Environment and Planning A: Economy and Space*, *55*(1), 72–99. https://doi.org/10.1177/0308518X211037688.

Alami, I., Dixon, A. D., Gonzalez-Vicente, R. et al. (2021). Geopolitics and the 'new' state capitalism. *Geopolitics*, *27*, 1–29. https://doi.org/10.1080/14650045.2021.1924943.

Alami, I., Dixon, A. D., & Mawdsley, E. (2021). State capitalism and the new global D/development regime. *Antipode*, *53*(5), 1294–318. https://doi.org/10.1111/anti.12725.

Aldane, J. (n.d.). *How capital is used makes a profound difference to the world we live in*. EDFI. 1 March, 2022, www.edfi.eu/interview/how-capital-is-used-makes-a-profound-difference-to-the-world-we-live-in/.

Altstedter, A. (2018, July 13). *Malaysia's IHH healthcare wins Fortis hospitals deal, beats TPG-backed Manipal.* Hindustan Times. www.hindustantimes .com/business-news/malaysia-s-ihh-healthcare-wins-fortis-hospitals-deal-beats-tpg-backed-manipal/story-WxdWx3Zhicf1EZmG4HD0BL.html.

Aron, R. (2009). *Bangkok's Bumrungrad hospital: Expanding the footprint of offshore health care.* Wharton School. https://knowledge.wharton.upenn .edu/article/bangkoks-bumrungrad-hospital-expanding-the-footprint-of-off shore-health-care/.

Arunanondchai, J., & Fink, C. (2006). Trade in health services in the ASEAN region. *Health Promotion International, 21*(suppl_1), 59–66. https://doi.org/ 10.1093/heapro/dal052.

Association of Bilateral European Development Finance Institutions. (2022). *Meet our members.* www.edfi.eu/members/meet-our-members/.

Baiterek. (2019, April 22). *Korean investors are expressing interest in PPP projects in Kazakhstan.* https://baiterek.gov.kz/en/pr/news/korean_investors_ are_expressing_interest_in_ppp_projects_in_kazakhstan0.

Balakrishnan, R., & Indulal PM. (2019a, October 23). *IHH plans to sell two assets in South India.* The Economic Times. https://economictimes.india times.com/industry/healthcare/biotech/healthcare/ihh-plans-to-sell-two-assets-in-south-india/articleshow/71715287.cms?from=mdr.

Balakrishnan, R., & Indulal PM. (2019b, May 27). *Medanta: Manipal hospitals to buy Medanta in Rs 5,800 crore deal.* The Economic Times. https://economic times.indiatimes.com/industry/healthcare/biotech/healthcare/manipal-hospitals-to-buy-medanta-in-rs-5800-crore-deal/articleshow/69509728.cms?from=mdr.

Balbuena, S. S. (2016). *Concerns related to the internationalisation of state-owned enterprises: Perspectives from regulators, government owners and the broader business community,* OECD Corporate Governance Working Papers 19. https://doi.org/10.1787/22230939.

Bartsch, S. (2009). Southern actors in global public-private partnerships: The case of the global fund. In S. J. Maclean, S. Brown, & P. Fourie (Eds.), *Health for Some: The Political Economy of Global Health Governance* (pp. 130–44). Palgrave Macmillan.

Baru, R. V. & Nundy M. (2020). *Commercialisation of Medical Care in China Changing Landscapes.* Routledge India.

Baru, R. V., & Jessani, A. (2000). The role of the World Bank in international health: Renewed commitment and partnership. *Social Science & Medicine, 50*(2), 183–4.

Bayliss, K., & Van Waeyenberge, E. (2017). Unpacking the public private partnership revival. *The Journal of Development Studies, 54*(4), 577–93. https://doi.org/10.1080/00220388.2017.1303671.

Bendavid, E., Ottersen, T., Peilong, L. et al. (2017). Development assistance for health. In Jamison D. T., Gelband H., Horton S. et al. (Eds.), *Disease Control Priorities, 3rd ed. (Volume 9): Improving Health and Reducing Poverty* (pp. 297–313). The World Bank. https://doi.org/10.1596/978-1-4648-0527-1_ch16.

Birn, A., Nervi, L., & Siqueira, E. (2016). Neoliberalism redux: The global health policy agenda and the politics of cooptation in Latin America and beyond. *Development and Change, 47*(4), 734–59. https://doi.org/10.1111/dech.12247.

Bremmer, I. (2009). State capitalism comes of age: The end of the free market? *Foreign Affairs, 88*(3), 40–55.

Brown, K. (2010, June 24). *Parkway bid report troubles investors.* Financial Times. www.ft.com/content/4273aa82-7fad-11df-91b4-00144feabdc0.

Brown, S. (2016). The instrumentalization of foreign aid under the Harper government. *Studies in Political Economy, 97*(1), 18–36. https://doi.org/10.1080/07078552.2016.1174461.

Brown, T. M., Cueto, M., & Fee, E. (2006). The World Health Organization and the transition from 'international' to 'global' public health. *American Journal of Public Health, 96*(1), 62–72. https://doi.org/10.2105/AJPH.2004.050831.

Buse, K., & Harmer, A. (2004). Power to the partners?: The politics of public-private health partnerships. *Development, 47*(2), 49–56. https://doi.org/10.1057/palgrave.development.1100029.

Buse, K., & Hawkes, S. (2015). Health in the sustainable development goals: Ready for a paradigm shift? *Globalization and Health, 11*(1), 13. https://doi.org/10.1186/s12992-015-0098-8.

Busfield, J. (2020). Documenting the financialisation of the pharmaceutical industry. *Social Science & Medicine, 258*, 113096. https://doi.org/10.1016/j.socscimed.2020.113096.

Business Standard. (2014, June 5). JBIC to invest into Takshasila hospitals. www.business-standard.com/article/economy-policy/jbic-to-invest-into-takshasila-hospitals-114060501021_1.html.

Business Wire. (2016, October 20). *GE invests in GAMA-TÜRKERLER JV to develop two major healthcare PPPs in Turkey; OPIC, EBRD and EDC to provide financing for transformational hospital project.* www.businesswire.com/news/home/20161020006211/en/GE-Invests-in-GAMA-TÜRKERLER-JV-to-Develop-Two-Major-Healthcare-PPPs-in-Turkey-OPIC-EBRD-and-EDC-to-Provide-Financing-for-Transformational-Hospital-Project.

Businesskorea. (2014, June 20). *K-Sure to guarantee high risk foreign project financing of KDB.* www.businesskorea.co.kr/news/articleView.html?idxno=5113.

Caldentey, E. P. (2008). The concept and evolution of the developmental state. *International Journal of Political Economy, 37*(3), 27–53. https://doi.org/10.2753/IJP0891-1916370302.

Campbell, D. (2019, September 12). *NHS hospital trusts to pay out further £55bn under PFI scheme.* The Guardian. www.theguardian.com/politics/2019/sep/12/nhs-hospital-trusts-to-pay-out-further-55bn-under-pfi-scheme.

Campbell, O., & Graham, W. (2006). Strategies for reducing maternal mortality: Getting on with what works. *Lancet, 368*(9543), 1284–99. https://doi.org/10.1016/S01406736(06)69381-1.

CDC Group. (2001). *Annual review 2001.*

CDC Group. (2017, June). *Healthcare global (Africa).* www.cdcgroup.com/en/our-impact/investment/healthcare-global/.

CDC Group. (2019). *Impact measurement: A practical guide to data collection.* https://assets.cdcgroup.com/wp-content/uploads/2019/12/04110848/CDC_ImpactMeasurementHandbook.pdf .

CDC Group. (2021a). *Catalyst strategies.* www.cdcgroup.com/en/our-approach/our-approach-to-investing/our-investment-solutions/catalyst-strategies/.

CDC Group. (2021b). *CDC's ESG toolkit.* https://toolkit.cdcgroup.com/.

CDC Group. (2021c). *Our investments.* www.cdcgroup.com/en/our-impact/search-results/?inv-sector%5B%5D=Health&inv-datefrom=&inv-dateto=.

CDC Group. (2021d, November 25). *Enlarged remit announced for the UK's development finance institution to deliver jobs and clean growth.* www.cdcgroup.com/en/news-insight/news/enlarged-remit-announced-for-the-uks-development-finance-institution-to-deliver-jobs-and-clean-growth/.

CDC Group. (2022). *Our history.* www.cdcgroup.com/en/about/our-history/.

CDC Group, & Department for International Development. (2019). *CDC group and DFID response.* https://assets.publishing.service.gov.uk/government/uploads/system/uploads/attachment_data/file/799977/CDC-investments-low-income-fragile-states-March2019.pdf.

Chan, L. H., Lee, P. K., & Chan, G. (2009). China engages global health governance: Processes and dilemmas. *Global Public Health, 4*(1), 1–30. https://doi.org/10.1080/17441690701524471.

Chandrashekhar, A. (2019, February 13). *Temasek makes Rs 270 crore investment in Dr Agarwal Eye Hospital for a minority stake.* The Economic Times. https://economictimes.indiatimes.com/small-biz/startups/newsbuzz/temasek-makes-rs-270-crore-investment-in-dr-agarwal-eye-hospital-for-a-minority-stake/articleshow/67975125.cms?from=mdr.

Chang, A. Y., Cowling, K., Micah, A. E. et al. (2019). Past, present, and future of global health financing: A review of development assistance, government, out-of-pocket, and other private spending on health for 195 countries, 1995–2050. *The Lancet*, *393*(10187), 2233–60. https://doi.org/10.1016/S0140-6736(19)30841-4.

Chee, H. L. (2008). Ownership, control, and contention: Challenges for the future of healthcare in Malaysia. *Social Science & Medicine*, *66*(10), 2145–56. https://doi.org/10.1016/j.socscimed.2008.01.036.

Chee, H. L. (2010). Medical tourism and the state in Malaysia and Singapore. *Global Social Policy: An Interdisciplinary Journal of Public Policy and Social Development*, *10*(3), 336–57. https://doi.org/10.1177/1468018110379978.

Cheng, Y., & Cheng, F. (2019). China's unique role in the field of global health. *Global Health Journal*, *3*(4), 98–101. https://doi.org/10.1016/j.glohj.2019.11.004.

Cho, J. (2014, December 1). *Samsung to build national hospital in Turkey.* BusinessKorea. www.businesskorea.co.kr/news/articleView.html?idxno=7552.

Choudhary, S., & Lim, K. (2010, July 25). *UPDATE 2-GIC defers preferential funding in India's Fortis.* Reuters. www.reuters.com/article/parkway-idINSGE65O04X20100625.

Clark, G., Dixon, A., & Monk, A. (2013). *Sovereign Wealth Funds: Legitimacy, Governance, and Global Power.* Princeton University Press. https://doi.org/10.1515/9781400846511.

Clark, S., & Louch, W. (2021). *The Key Man: How the Global Elite was Duped by a Capitalist Fairy Tale.* Penguin.

Clarke, G. (2018). UK development policy and domestic politics 1997–2016. *Third World Quarterly*, *39*(1), 18–34. https://doi.org/10.1080/01436597.2017.1369032.

Clay, E. J., Geddes, M., & Natali, L. (2009). *Untying aid: Is it working? An Evaluation of the implementation of the Paris declaration and of the 2001 DAC recommendation of untying ODA to the LDCs.* https://www.oecd.org/development/evaluation/dcdndep/44375975.pdf.

CNN. (2003, October 21). Mayne sells hospitals for $561m. *CNN.Com.* http://edition.cnn.com/2003/BUSINESS/10/20/australia.mayne.biz/.

Cooper, A., Kirton, J., & Schrecker, T. (2007). *Governing Global Health: Challenge, Response, Innovation.* Routledge.

Coyne, C. J., & Williamson, C. R. (2014). Can international aid improve health? In G. W. Brown, G. Yamey, & S. Wamala (Eds.), *The Handbook of Global Health Policy* (pp. 375–92). Wiley-Blackwell.

Cuervo-Cazurra, A. (2018). Thanks but no thanks: State-owned multinationals from emerging markets and host-country policies. *Journal of*

International Business Policy, *1*(3–4), 128–56. https://doi.org/10.1057/s42214-018-0009-9.

Cumhuriyet. (2011, May 25). Erdoğan Ankara projesini açıkladı. *Cumhuriyet*. www.cumhuriyet.com.tr/haber/erdogan-ankara-projesini-acikladi-251954.

Das, A. (2016, March 28). *Kirloskar sells stake in Sakra Hosp*. Times of India. https://timesofindia.indiatimes.com/business/india-business/kirloskar-sells-stake-in-sakra-hosp/articleshow/51577452.cms.

Davis, T. W. D. (2011). Foreign aid in Australia's relationship with the South: Institutional narratives. *The Round Table*, *100*(415), 389–406. https://doi.org/10.1080/00358533.2011.595254.

Department for International Development. (2011, June 7). *Andrew Mitchell on the reform of CDC Group plc*. www.gov.uk/government/speeches/andrew-mitchell-on-the-reform-of-cdc-group-plc.

Dieleman, J. L., Schneider, M. T., Haakenstad, A. et al. (2016). Development assistance for health: Past trends, associations, and the future of international financial flows for health. *The Lancet*, *387*(10037), 2536–44. https://doi.org/10.1016/S0140-6736(16)30168-4.

Dixon, A. D. (2022). The strategic logics of state investment funds in Asia: Beyond financialisation. *Journal of Contemporary Asia*, *52*(1), 127–51. https://doi.org/10.1080/00472336.2020.1841267.

Doherty, J. (2011). *Expansion of the private health sector in east and Southern Africa*. EQUINET Discussion Paper 87. University of the Witwatersrand. https://equinetafrica.org/sites/default/files/uploads/documents/EQ_Diss_87_Private_HS.pdf.

Douglass, M. (1994). The 'developmental state' and the newly industrialised economies of Asia. *Environment and Planning A: Economy and Space*, *26*(4), 543–66. https://doi.org/10.1068/a260543.

Economic Times. (2017, May 19). *Khazanah unit offloads its entire stake in Apollo Hospitals for Rs 850 cr*. https://economictimes.indiatimes.com/markets/stocks/news/khazanah-unit-offloads-its-entire-stake-in-apollo-hospitals-for-rs-850-cr/articleshow/58745502.cms?from=mdr.

Elekta. (1999). *Annual report 1998/1999*.

Elekta. (2001). *Annual report 2000/01*.

Epstein, G. (2005). *Financialization and the World Economy*. Edward Elgar.

Eren Vural, I. (2017). Financialisation in health care: An analysis of private equity fund investments in Turkey. *Social Science & Medicine*, *187*, 276–86. https://doi.org/10.1016/j.socscimed.2017.06.008.

Ethiopia Observer. (2018, May 11). *Charges dropped against heart surgeon Fikru Maru*. www.ethiopiaobserver.com/2018/05/11/charges-dropped-against-heart-surgeon-fikru-maru/.

Eurodad. (2018). *History repeated: How public private partnerships are failing.* https://assets.nationbuilder.com/eurodad/pages/508/attachments/original/1590679608/How_Public_Private_Partnerships_are_failing.pdf?1590679608.

Evans, S. (2005). *Ramsay, Affinity hop into bed.* The Australian Financial Review. www.afr.com/companies/ramsay-affinity-hop-into-bed-20050415-jl57j.

Export-Import Bank of Korea. (2021). *About the bank | vision and value.* www.koreaexim.go.kr/site/homepage/menu/viewMenu?menuid=002001003001.

Feeny, S., & Ouattara, B. (2013). The effects of health aid on child health promotion in developing countries: Cross-country evidence. *Applied Economics*, *45*(7), 911–19. https://doi.org/10.1080/00036846.2011.613779.

Financial Times. (2010, July 1). *Parkway hospitals. A tussle is developing over Asia's biggest play on medical tourism.* www.ft.com/content/d90f66a4-84ec-11df-adfa-00144feabdc0.

Financial Times. (2020). *American shared hospital services announces acquisition of gamma knife center, Ecuador S.A.* https://markets.ft.com/data/announce/full?dockey=1330-7947090en-652TC2I3U2E1L875LLBI346S9A.

Financial Tribune. (2015, October 5). *S. Korean firms scour Iran for business opportunities.* https://financialtribune.com/articles/economy-business-and-markets/27329/s-korean-firms-scour-iran-for-business-opportunities.

Financial Tribune. (2016, May 11). *Foreign firms investing in Iran health projects.* https://financialtribune.com/articles/people/41302/foreign-firms-investing-in-iran-health-projects.

FMO. (1998). *Agreement state-FMO of 16 November 1998.*

FMO. (2005). *Annual report 2004.*

FMO. (2012). *Annual report 2011.*

FMO. (2013). *Annual report 2012.*

FMO. (2015a). *Annual report 2014.*

FMO. (2015b, May 6). *Project detail – IFHA-II COOPERATIEF U.A.* www.fmo.nl/project-detail/43060.

FMO. (2015c, December 16). *FMO supports healthcare in Africa.* www.fmo.nl/news-detail/f31f22de-9c28-49ba-8132-bd5507f00f9a/fmo-supports-healthcare-in-africa.

FMO. (2016). *Annual report 2015.*

FMO. (2019). *NedLinx BV.* https://annualreport.fmo.nl/2018/reports/ar2018/corporate-governance-1/nedlinx-bv.

FMO. (2020a). *Annual report 2019.*

FMO. (2020b). *Development accelerator: Annual report 2019.*

FMO. (2021a). *Development accelerator: Annual report 2020.*

FMO. (2021b). *Invest international starts financing Dutch solutions for global challenges.* www.fmo.nl/news-detail/14511c8c-a777-4318-b1b1-5eae73292fdd/invest-international-starts-financing-dutch-solutions-for-glo bal-challenges.

FMO. (2022a). *Annual report 2021.*

FMO. (2022b). *Funding: Investor relations.* www.fmo.nl/invest-with-us/funding.

Gabor, D. (2021). The wall street consensus. *Development and Change, 52*(3), 429–59. https://doi.org/10.1111/dech.12645.

Gabriel, A. (2010, July 31). *Battle for parkway.* The Star. www.thestar.com.my/business/business-news/2010/07/31/battle-for-parkway.

Gautier, L., De Allegri, M., & Ridde, V. (2019). How is the discourse of performance-based financing shaped at the global level? A poststructural analysis. *Globalization and Health, 15*(1), 6. https://doi.org/10.1186/s12992-018-0443-9.

Gaziantep Special Purpose Vehicle. (2021). *Gaziantep integrated health campus.* http://gaziantepihcproject.com/english.

Ghana National Association of Teachers. (2021). *The Sweden Ghana Medical Centre (SGMC).* www.ghanateachers.com/new/divisions/our-subsidiaries/sgmc-cancer-center.

Ghosh, D. (2021, May 10). *Ranjan Pai: Building a healthcare empire.* Fortune India. www.fortuneindia.com/enterprise/ranjan-pai-building-a-healthcare-empire/105470.

GIC. (2013). *Report on the management of the government's portfolio for the Year 2012/13.* www.gic.com.sg/wp-content/uploads/2021/03/GIC_Report_2013.pdf.

GIC. (2014, May 16). *GIC invests in minority stake to expand MPIC hospital group.* www.gic.com.sg/newsroom/news/gic-invests-in-minority-stake-to-expand-mpic-hospital-group/.

GIC. (2019, October 15). *MPIC raises Php 35.3bn from co-investment by GIC and KKR in hospital unit.* www.gic.com.sg/newsroom/news/mpic-raises-php-35-3bn-from-co-investment-by-gic-and-kkr-in-hospital-unit/.

GIC. (2021, June 24). *GIC invests RM750 million in Sunway healthcare.* www.gic.com.sg/newsroom/all/gic-invests-rm750-million-in-sunway-healthcare/.

Gideon, J., Hunter, B. M., & Murray, S. F. (2017). Public-private partnerships in sexual and reproductive healthcare provision: Establishing a gender analysis. *Journal of International and Comparative Social Policy, 33*(2), 166–80. https://doi.org/10.1080/21699763.2017.1329157.

Gideon, J., & Unterhalter, E. (2017). Exploring public private partnerships in health and education: A critique. *Journal of International and Comparative*

Social Policy, *33*(2), 136–41. https://doi.org/10.1080/21699763.2017 .1330699.

Gill, I. (2018, January 19). *The end of aid*. Future development. www.brook ings.edu/blog/future-development/2018/01/19/the-end-of-aid/.

Global Justice Now. (2020). *Doing more harm than good: Why CDC must reform for people and planet*. www.globaljustice.org.uk/wp-content/uploads/ 2020/02/web_gjn_-_doing_more_harm_than_good_cdc_-_feb_2020_2.pdf.

Gomez, E. (2009). The politics of receptivity and resistance: How Brazil, India, China, and Russia strategically use the international health community in response to HIV/AIDS: A Theory. *Global Health Governance*, *3*(1), 1–29.

Gooptu, B. (2013, December 19). *Quadria capital-led investor consortium picks up majority stake in Medica Synergie*. The Economic Times. https:// economictimes.indiatimes.com/industry/healthcare/biotech/healthcare/quad ria-capital-led-investor-consortium-picks-up-majority-stake-in-medica-synergie/articleshow/27654347.cms?from=mdr.

Government of Japan. (2013). *Japan revitalization strategy: Japan is back*.

Government of Japan. (2014). *The healthcare policy*.

Government of Kenya. (2019). *SDG partnership platform*.

Government of Turkey. (2021). *Investing in infrastructure & Public Private Partnership (PPP) projects in Turkey?*

Grant, J. (2012, July 3). *IHH extends Malaysia's big-ticket IPO run*. Financial Times. www.ft.com/content/21c80f3a-c4d4-11e1-b8fd-00144feabdc0.

Gray, K., & Gills, B. K. (2016). South–South cooperation and the rise of the Global South. *Third World Quarterly*, *37*(4), 557–74. https://doi.org/10.1080/ 01436597.2015.1128817.

Greenblat, E. (2005). *Affinity health eyes Asian expansion*. The Australian Financial Review. www.afr.com/companies/affinity-health-eyes-asian-expan sion-20050228-jl8ro.

Grépin, K. A., Fan, V. Y., Shen, G. C., & Chen, L. (2014). China's role as a global health donor in Africa: what can we learn from studying under reported resource flows? *Globalization and Health*, *10*(1), 84. https://doi .org/10.1186/s12992-014-0084-6.

Griffith-Jones, S., & Ocampo, J. A. (2018). *The Future of National Development Banks* (S. Griffith-Jones & J. A. Ocampo, Eds., Vol. 1). Oxford University Press. https://doi.org/10.1093/oso/9780198827948 .001.0001

Guillon, J. (2021). How a modern private hospital was created in Vietnam. *Magazine Des Professions Financières et de l'Économie*. www.professionsfi nancieres.com/How-a-modern-private-hospital-was-created-in-Vietnam.

Gulrajani, N. (2017). Bilateral donors and the age of the national interest: What prospects for challenge by development agencies? *World Development*, *96*, 375–89.

Hamer, J., & Kapilashrami, A. (2020). Win-win collaboration?: Understanding donor-private sector engagement in health and its implications for Universal Health Coverage. In J. Gideon & E. Unterhalter (Eds.), *Critical Reflections on Public Private Partnerships* (pp. 214–32). Routledge.

Harman, S. (2009). The world bank and health. In A. Kay & O. D. Williams (Eds.), *Global Health Governance: Crisis, Institutions and Political Economy* (pp. 227–44). Palgrave Macmillan.

Harman, S. (2012). *Global Health Governance*. Routledge.

Harman, S. (2016). The Bill and Melinda Gates Foundation and legitimacy in global health governance. *Global Governance: A Review of Multilateralism and International Organizations*, *22*(3), 349–68.

Harmer, A., & Buse, K. (2014). The BRICS – A paradigm shift in global health? *Contemporary Politics*, *20*(2), 127–45. https://doi.org/10.1080/13569775.2014.907988.

Harvey, D. (2005). *A Brief History of Neoliberalism*. Oxford University Press.

Hayes, M. (2016, May 20). *Korean firms in for US$ 2 bn hospitals projects in Iran*. KHL. www.khl.com/news/korean-firms-in-for-us-2-bn-hospitals-projects-in-iran/1118136.article.

Herzer, D. (2019). The long-run effect of aid on health: Evidence from panel cointegration analysis. *Applied Economics*, *51*(12), 1319–38. https://doi.org/10.1080/00036846.2018.1527449.

Heymann, D. L., Chen, L., Takemi, K. et al. (2015). Global health security: The wider lessons from the West African Ebola virus disease epidemic. *The Lancet*, *385*(9980), 1884–901. https://doi.org/10.1016/S0140-6736(15)60858-3.

Hindustan Times. (2010, May 10). *Fortis health to raise Rs 380 crore*.www.hindustantimes.com/business/fortis-health-to-raise-rs-380-crore/story-yIVCMRwwdtqy1jJMGZxGKK.html.

HM Treasury. (2015). *UK aid: Tackling global challenges in the national interest*. https://assets.publishing.service.gov.uk/government/uploads/system/uploads/attachment_data/file/478834/ODA_strategy_final_web_0905.pdf.

Hochstetler, K., & Montero, A. P. (2013). The renewed developmental state: The National Development Bank and the Brazil model. *Journal of Development Studies*, *49*(11), 1484–99. https://doi.org/10.1080/00220388.2013.807503.

Hoffman, S. J., & Cole, C. B. (2018). Defining the global health system and systematically mapping its network of actors. *Globalization and Health*, *14*(1), 38. https://doi.org/10.1186/s12992-018-0340-2.

Honeyman, V. C. (2019). New Labour's overseas development aid policy–charity or self-interest? *Contemporary British History, 33*(3), 313–35. https://doi.org/10.1080/13619462.2018.1544498.

Hospital Management. (2017, June 20). *EBRD grants €80m loan to construct new hospital in Gaziantep, Turkey.* www.hospitalmanagement.net/news/newsebrd-grants-80m-loan-to-construct-new-hospital-in-gaziantep-turkey-5850222/.

House of Commons International Development Committee. (2011). *The future of CDC.* https://publications.parliament.uk/pa/cm201011/cmselect/cmintdev/607/607.pdf.

Huang, Y. (2020). Emerging powers and global health governance. In C. McInnes, K. Lee, & J. Youde (Eds.), *The Oxford Handbook of Global Health Politics* (pp. 299–324). Oxford University Press. https://doi.org/10.1093/oxfordhb/9780190456818.013.19_update_001.

Hughes-McLure, S., & Mawdsley, E. (2022). Innovative finance for development? Vaccine bonds and the hidden costs of financialization. *Economic Geography, 98*(2), 145–69. https://doi.org/10.1080/00130095.2021.2020090.

Humania. (2022). *Humania, making a difference.* www.humaniacap.com/about-us/.

Hunter, B. M., Bisht, R., & Murray, S. F. (2020). Neoliberalisation enacted through development aid: The case of health vouchers in India. *Critical Public Health, 32*(2), 193–205. https://doi.org/10.1080/09581596.2020.1770695.

Hunter, B. M., Harrison, S., Portela, A., & Bick, D. (2017). The effects of cash transfers and vouchers on the use and quality of maternity care services: A systematic review. *PLoS ONE, 12*(3). https://doi.org/10.1371/journal.pone.0173068.

Hunter, B. M., & Marriott, A. (2018). Development finance institutions and the (in)coherence of their investments in private healthcare companies. In B. Tomlinson, E. R. Palomares, & L. A. Pano (Eds.), *The Reality of Aid 2018* (pp. 33–44). IBON International.

Hunter, B. M., & Murray, S. F. (2015). 'Beyond aid' investments in private healthcare in developing countries. *BMJ, 3012*(July), h3012. https://doi.org/10.1136/bmj.h3012.

Hunter, B. M., & Murray, S. F. (2019). Deconstructing the financialization of healthcare. *Development and Change, 50*(5), 1263–87. https://doi.org/10.1111/dech.12517.

Hunter, B. M., Murray, S. F., Marathe, S., & Chakravarthi, I. (2022). Decentred regulation: The case of private healthcare in India. *World Development, 155*, 105889. https://doi.org/10.1016/j.worlddev.2022.105889

Husain, L., & Bloom, G. (2020). Understanding China's growing involvement in global health and managing processes of change. *Globalization and Health*, *16*(1), 39. https://doi.org/10.1186/s12992-020-00569-0.

IFC. (2008a). *IFC investment to help expand high-quality health care, retain medical talent, and create employment in the Philippines.* https://pressroom .ifc.org/all/pages/PressDetail.aspx?ID=22245.

IFC. (2008b). *The business of health in Africa.* https://documents1.worldbank .org/curated/en/878891468002994639/pdf/441430WP0ENGLI1an101 10200801PUBLIC1.pdf.

IFC. (2013, July 2). *IFC invests in AAR to improve health services in East Africa.* https://pressroom.ifc.org/all/pages/PressDetail.aspx?ID=15409.

IFC. (2014a, February 17). *IFHA II.* https://disclosures.ifc.org/project-detail/ SII/34034/ifha-ii.

IFC. (2014b, December 15). *IFC invests $255 million in Rede D'Or to expand access to healthcare services in Brazil.* https://pressroom.ifc.org/all/pages/ PressDetail.aspx?ID=17168.

IFC. (2015). *Turkey: Turkish healthcare PPP program Adana hospital complex.* https://documents1.worldbank.org/curated/en/925991484654860294/pdf/ 111339-PPPStories-TurkeyAdanaHospitalComplex.pdf.

IHH Healthcare Berhad. (2012). *IHH healthcare Berhad prospectus.* www .insage.com.my/Upload/Docs/IHH/IHH%20Prospectus%202012.pdf.

IHME. (2022). *Financing global health.* https://vizhub.healthdata.org/fgh/.

Ikitelli Integrated Health Campus Project. (2016). *About project.* www.pppiki tellihastanesi.com/en/29594/About-Project.

InfraPPP. (2015). *Ronesans holding acquires Istanbul Ikitelli hospital PPP in Turkey.* www.infrapppworld.com/news/megaproject-528-ronesans-holding-acquires-istanbul-ikitelli-hospital-ppp-in-turkey.

InfraPPP. (2016). *Financiers announced for Turkish hospital PPP.* www.infrapppworld.com/news/financiers-announced-for-turkish-hospital-ppp.

InfraPPP. (2017, May 18). *New investor joins sponsors of Gaziantep hospital PPP.* www.infrapppworld.com/news/megaproject-930-new-investor-joins-sponsors-of-gaziantep-hospital-ppp.

Institute for Health Metrics and Evaluation. (2019). *Development assistance for health database 1990–2018.* https://doi.org/10.6069/M8B5-FE25.

Invest International. (2022). *About us.* https://investinternational.nl/about-us/ background/.

Investment Fund for Health in Africa. (2022). *Portfolio.* www.ifhafund.com/ portfolio-companies/portfolio/.

Investors for Health. (2021). *Investors for health.* www.investorsforhealth.com/.

Janus, H., Klingebiel, S., & Paulo, S. (2015). Beyond aid: A conceptual perspective on the transformation of development cooperation. *Journal of International Development*, *27*(2), 155–69. https://doi.org/10.1002/jid.3045.

Jayaseelan, R. (2010, July 31). *Parkway's long history with Malaysia*. The Star. www.thestar.com.my/business/business-news/2010/07/31/parkways-long-history-with-malaysia/.

JBIC. (2014, June 5). *Equity participation in India's Takshasila hospitals operating private limited*. www.jbic.go.jp/en/information/press/press-2014/0605-21920.html.

JBIC. (2017, July 21). *Project finance and political risk guarantee for Ikitelli hospital PPP project in the Republic of Turkey*. www.jbic.go.jp/en/information/press/press-2017/0721-56156.html.

JBIC. (2019). *JBIC profile: Role and function*. www.jbic.go.jp/en/about/role-function.html.

JBIC. (2021, January). Using collaborations with overseas companies to drive the realization of society 5.0. *JBIC Today*. www.jbic.go.jp/en/information/today/today-2020/contents/jtd_202101.pdf.

JICA. (2015). *Preparatory survey on hospital establishment project in Aydin province: Final report*. https://openjicareport.jica.go.jp/pdf/12244620.pdf.

JICA. (2016). *Data collection survey for introduction of Japanese expertise on hospital PPP project in the Republic of Turkey: Final Report*. https://openjicareport.jica.go.jp/pdf/12254421.pdf.

Johnson, C. (1982). *MITI and the Japanese Miracle: The Growth of Industrial Policy, 1925–1975*. Stanford University Press.

Johnson, J. (2015, January 19). *Temasek buys 18% stake in Medanta from Punj Lloyd*. VCCircle. www.vccircle.com/temasek-buys-18-stake-medanta-punj-lloyd.

Jubilee Debt Campaign. (2017). *Double standards: How the UK promotes rip-off health PPPs abroad*. www.jubileedebt.org.uk/doublestandards.

Kapilashrami, A., & Baru, R. (2018). *Global Health Governance and Commercialisation in India*. Routledge.

Katada, S. N. (2002). Japan's two-track aid approach: The forces behind competing triads. *Asian Survey*, *42*(2), 320–42. https://doi.org/10.1525/as.2002.42.2.320.

Kay, A., & Williams, O. D. (2009). *Global Health Governance : Crisis, Institutions and Political Economy*. Palgrave Macmillan.

Keijzer, N., & Lundsgaarde, E. (2018). When 'unintended effects' reveal hidden intentions: Implications of 'mutual benefit' discourses for evaluating development cooperation. *Evaluation and Program Planning*, *68*, 210–17. https://doi.org/10.1016/j.evalprogplan.2017.09.003.

Keshavjee, S. (2014). *Blind Spot: How Neoliberalism Infiltrated Global Health.* University of California Press.

Khazanah Nasional. (2010). *Khazanah and Integrated Healthcare Holdings Sdn Bhd, via its wholly owned subsidiary Integrated Healthcare Holdings Limited, announces the successful close of its voluntary general offer for Parkway Holdings Limited.* Press Release. www.khazanah.com.my/news_press_re leases/khazanah-and-integrated-healthcare-holdings-sdn-bhd-via-its-wholly-owned-subsidiary-integrated-healthcare-holdings-limited-announces-the-suc cessful-close-of-its-voluntary-general-offer-for-parkway-h/.

Khazanah Nasional Berhad. (2005). *Khazanah acquires stake in Apollo hospitals enterprise limited.* Press Release. www.khazanah.com.my/news_ press_releases/khazanah-acquires-stake-in-apollo-hospitals-enterprise-limited/.

Khazanah Nasional Berhad. (2006). *Khazanah acquires a substantial stake In Pantai holdings berhad and to set up a joint venture with Parkway holdings ltd. and launch mandatory offer for Pantai shares.* Press Release. www .khazanah.com.my/news_press_releases/khazanah-acquires-a-substantial-stake-in-pantai-holdings-berhad-and-to-set-up-a-joint-venture-with-park way-holdings-ltd-and-laun-ch-mandatory-offer-for-pantai-shares/.

Khazanah Nasional Berhad. (2021). *Our history.* www.khazanah.com.my/who-we-are/our-history/.

Kickbusch, I. (2012). Addressing the interface of the political and commercial determinants of health. *Health Promotion International, 27*(4), 427–8. https://doi.org/10.1093/heapro/das057.

Kickbusch, I., & Kokeny, M. (2013). Global health diplomacy: Five years on. *Bull World Health Organ, 91*(3), 159–159A. https://doi.org/10.2471/BLT.13 .118596.

Kickbusch, I., & Szabo, M. M. C. (2014). A new governance space for health. *Global Health Action, 7*(1), 23507. https://doi.org/10.3402/gha.v7.23507.

Kim, D. (2018, January 19). KDB infra invests $60 mn in Turkey's hospital PPP debt. *The Korea Economic Daily.* www.jubileedebt.org.uk/doublestandards.

Kim, J. (2015). *Hong pledges to reinvent KDB.* The Korea Times. www .koreatimes.co.kr/www/biz/2021/11/488_192057.html.

King, N. B., & Koski, A. (2020). Defining global health as public health somewhere else. *BMJ Global Health, 5*(1), e002172. https://doi.org/ 10.1136/bmjgh-2019-002172.

Klitzing, E., Lin, D., Lund, S., & Nordin, L. (2010). Demystifying sovereign wealth funds. In S. Das, A. Mazarei, & H. van der Hoorn (Eds.), *Economics of Sovereign Wealth Funds: Issues for Policymakers* (pp. 3–14). International Monetary Fund.

Krech, R., Kickbusch, I., Franz, C., & Wells, N. (2018). Banking for health: The role of financial sector actors in investing in global health. *BMJ Global Health, 3*(Suppl 1), e000597. https://doi.org/10.1136/bmjgh-2017-000597.

Kring, W. N., & Gallagher, K. P. (2019). Strengthening the foundations? Alternative institutions for finance and development. *Development and Change, 50*(1), 3–23. https://doi.org/10.1111/dech.12464.

Kumar, R. (2019). Public–private partnerships for universal health coverage? The future of 'free health' in Sri Lanka. *Globalization and Health, 15*(S1), 75. https://doi.org/10.1186/s12992-019-0522-6.

Kurian, B. (2017, September 18). *Temasek buys Rs 1k-cr Manipal stake*. Times of India. https://timesofindia.indiatimes.com/business/india-business/tema sek-buys-rs-1k-cr-manipal-stake/articleshow/60724907.cms

Lakoff, A. (2010). Two regimes of global health. *Humanity: An International Journal of Human Rights, Humanitarianism, and Development, 1*(1), 59–79. https://doi.org/10.1353/hum.2010.0001.

Lakoff, A. (2017). *Unprepared: Global Health in a Time of Emergency.* University of California Press.

Languille, S. (2017). Public private partnerships in education and health in the global South: A literature review. *Journal of International and Comparative Social Policy, 33*(2), 1–24. https://doi.org/10.1080/21699763.2017.1307779.

Lee, K. (2019). Financing Industrial Development in Korea and Implications for Africa. In C. Monga & J. Y. Lin (Eds.), *The Oxford Handbook of Structural Transformation* (pp. 549–70). Oxford University Press.

Lee, L., & Daga, A. (2018, November 29). *Malaysia's Khazanah cuts IHH holding with $2 billion stake sale to Mitsui.* Reuters. www.reuters.com/article/us-ihh-m-a-mitsui-co-idUSKCN1NY0AF.

Lefebvre, B. (2010). *Hospital chains in India: Coming of age?* www.ifri.org/sites/default/files/atoms/files/asievisions23blefebvre.pdf.

Lethbridge, J. (2015). *Health care reforms and the rise of global multinational health care companies.* www.ifri.org/sites/default/files/atoms/files/asievi sions23blefebvre.pdf.

Lethbridge, J. (2016). *Unhealthy development: The UK department for international development and the promotion of healthcare privatisation.* www .ifri.org/sites/default/files/atoms/files/asievisions23blefebvre.pdf.

Lisk, F., & Šehović, A. B. (2020). Rethinking global health governance in a changing world order for achieving sustainable development: The role and potential of the 'rising powers'. *Fudan Journal of the Humanities and Social Sciences, 13*(1), 45–65. https://doi.org/10.1007/s40647-018-00250-2.

Lunt, N. (2017). Exporting healthcare services: A comparative discussion of the UK, Turkey and South Korea. In D. Horsfall & J. Hudson (Eds.), *Social

Policy in an Era of Competition (pp. 103–16). Policy Press. https://doi.org/
10.51952/9781447326298.ch006.

Mackintosh, M., Channon, A., Karan, A. et al. (2016). What is the private
sector? Understanding private provision in the health systems of low-income
and middle-income countries. *The Lancet, 388*(10044), 596–605. https://doi
.org/10.1016/S0140-6736(16)00342-1.

Maclean, S. J., Brown, S. A., & Fourie, P. (2009). *Health for Some: The
Political Economy of Global Health Governance*. Palgrave Macmillan.

Mader, P., Mertens, D., & van der Zwan, N. (2020). *The Routledge International
Handbook of Financialization*. Routledge.

Mah, L. (2018). *Promoting private sector for development: The rise of blended
finance in EU aid architecture*. www.repository.utl.pt/bitstream/10400.5/
16301/1/wp171.pdf.

Mahajan, M. (2018). Philanthropy and the nation-state in global health: The
Gates Foundation in India. *Global Public Health, 13*(10), 1357–68. https://
doi.org/10.1080/17441692.2017.1414286.

Mahajan, M. (2019). The IHME in the shifting landscape of global health
metrics. *Global Policy, 10*(S1), 110–20. https://doi.org/10.1111/1758-
5899.12605.

Marathe, S., Hunter, B. M., Chakravarthi, I., Shukla, A., & Murray, S. F. (2020).
The impacts of corporatisation of healthcare on medical practice and profes-
sionals in Maharashtra, India. *BMJ Global Health, 5*(2), e002026. https://doi
.org/10.1136/bmjgh-2019-002026.

Marriott, A., & Hamer, J. (2014). *Investing for the few: The IFC's health in
Africa initiative*. https://oxfamilibrary.openrepository.com/bitstream/handle/
10546/325654/bn-investing-for-few-ifc-health-in-africa-100914-en.pdf;
jsessionid=0763F39D70B44D949738A6B6D6A904D5?sequence=1.

Mawdsley, E. (2016). Development geography II: Financialization. *Progress in
Human Geography, 42*(2), 264–74. https://doi.org/10.1177/0309132516
678747.

Mawdsley, E. (2017). National interests and the paradox of foreign aid under
austerity: Conservative governments and the domestic politics of international development since 2010. *The Geographical Journal, 183*(3), 223–
32. https://doi.org/10.1111/geoj.12219.

Mawdsley, E., Murray, W. E., Overton, J., Scheyvens, R., & Banks, G. (2018).
Exporting stimulus and 'shared prosperity': Reinventing foreign aid for
a retroliberal era. *Development Policy Review, 36*, O25–O43. https://doi
.org/10.1111/dpr.12282.

Mawdsley, E., Savage, L., & Kim, S.-M. (2014). A "post-aid world"? Paradigm
shift in foreign aid and development cooperation at the 2011 Busan High

Level Forum. *The Geographical Journal*, *180*(1), 27–38. https://doi.org/10.1111/j.1475-4959.2012.00490.x.

Mawdsley, E., & Taggart, J. (2022). Rethinking d/Development. *Progress in Human Geography*, *46*(1), 3–20. https://doi.org/10.1177/03091325211053115.

McCoy, D., & McGoey, L. (2011). Global health and the gates foundation – In perspective. In S. Rushton & O. Williams (Eds.), *Partnerships and Foundations in Global Health Governance* (pp. 143–63). Palgrave Macmillan.

McGoey, L. (2015). *No Such Thing as a Free Gift: The Gates Foundation and the Price of Philanthropy*. Verso Books.

McInnes, C., Kamradt-Scott, A., Lee, K. et al. (2014). *The Transformation of Global Health Governance*. Palgrave Macmillan.

Medical Credit Fund. (2014). *Philips and Medical Credit Fund announce partnership*. www.medicalcreditfund.org/update/philips-and-medical-credit-fund-announce-partnership/.

Medical Credit Fund. (2021). *Medical Credit Fund raises EUR 32.5 million to support health entrepreneurs in sub-Saharan Africa*. www.medicalcreditfund.org/update/medical-credit-fund-raises-eur-32-5-million-to-support-health-entrepreneurs-in-sub-saharan-africa/.

Medical Dialogues. (2019, June 12). *Eye care chain Disha medical services raises over Rs 27 crore in series C funding*. https://business.medicaldialogues.in/eye-care-chain-disha-medical-services-raises-over-rs-27-crore-in-series-c-funding.

Medical Excellence Japan. (2019). *Implementation of projects commissioned by governmental agencies*. https://medicalexcellencejapan.org/en/entrustment/index.php#entrustment-1.

Micah, A. E., Zhao, Y., Chen, C. S. et al. (2019). Tracking development assistance for health from China, 2007–2017. *BMJ Global Health*, *4*(5), e001513. https://doi.org/10.1136/bmjgh-2019-001513.

Mills, A. (2014). Health care systems in low- and middle-income countries. *New England Journal of Medicine*, *370*(6), 552–7. https://doi.org/10.1056/NEJMra1110897.

Milward, H. B., & Provan, K. G. (2000). Governing the hollow state. *Journal of Public Administration Research and Theory*, *10*(2), 359–80.

Ministry of Health and Welfare. (2019, April 23). *Korea accelerating healthcare cooperation with Central Asian countries*. www.mohw.go.kr/eng/nw/nw0101vw.jsp?PAR_MENU_ID=1007&MENU_ID=100701&page=6&CONT_SEQ=349164.

Mint. (2016, May 30). *Multiples PE puts Vikram hospital stake on sale*. www.livemint.com/Companies/Z8Ki3i5hpAPaxsXF3fceCL/Multiples-PE-puts-Vikram-Hospital-stake-on-sale.html.

Mint. (2020, November 3). *Manipal buys Columbia for ₹1,800 crore.* www
.livemint.com/companies/news/manipal-health-to-acquire-100-stake-in-col
umbia-asia-hospitals-11604300192775.html.

Mitsui. (2011, December 26). *Mitsui & Co. associated company integrated
healthcare holdings to acquire stake in Turkish healthcare group.* www
.mitsui.com/jp/en/release/2011/1205173_6470.html.

Mohan, G., & Mawdsley, E. (2007). The war on terror, American hegemony and
international development. *Review of International Political Economy, 14*(3),
439–43. https://doi.org/10.1080/09692290701395692.

Monetary Authority of Singapore. (1998). *Fund management in Singapore: New
directions | speech by Deputy Prime Minister Lee Hsien Loong, at the invest-
ment Management Association of Singapore seminar.* www.mas.gov.sg/news/
speeches/1998/fund-management-in-singapore-new-directions–26-feb-1998.

Morrison, D. (1998). *Aid and Ebb Tide: A History of CIDA and Canadian
Development Assistance.* Wilfrid Laurier University Press.

Morrison, J. (2012). *The end of the golden era of global health?* www.csis.org/
analysis/end-golden-era-global-health

Musacchio, A., Lazzarini, S., Makhoul, P., & Simmons, E. (2017). *The role and
impact of development banks.* https://people.brandeis.edu/~aldom/papers/
The%20Role%20and%20Impact%20of%20Development%20Banks%20-%
203-9-2017.pdf.

Naqvi, A. (2016, May). Partnership capital can solve global development
challenges. *Institutional Investor Magazine.* www.institutionalinvestor.com/
article/b14z9qp29sksm8/partnership-capital-can-solve-global-development-
challenges.

Ngui, Y., & Kok, C. (2012, July 25). *Malaysia's IHH jumps 14 percent as
world's No.3 IPO debuts.* Reuters. www.reuters.com/article/us-malaysia-ihh-
ipo-idUSBRE86O03J20120725.

Nishigaki, A. (2000). A new phase in Japanese economic cooperation. *Asia-
Pacific Review, 7*(1), 56–65. https://doi.org/10.1080/713650814.

OECD. (2015). *State-owned enterprises in the development process.* www
.oecd.org/corporate/state-owned-enterprises-in-the-development-process-
9789264229617-en.htm.

OECD. (2016). *Dutch Good Growth Fund (DGGF), Netherlands enterprise
agency.*

OECD. (2021). *COVID-19 spending helped to lift foreign aid to an all-time high
in 2020.*

OECD. (2022a). *Development finance institutions and private sector development.* www.oecd.org/development/development-finance-institutions-private-
sector-development.htm.

OECD. (2022b). *History of DAC lists of aid recipient countries.* www.oecd.org/ dac/financing-sustainable-development/development-finance-standards/his toryofdaclistsofaidrecipientcountries.htm.

OECD. (2022c). *Official Development Assistance (ODA).* www.oecd.org/dac/ financing-sustainable-development/development-finance-standards/official- development-assistance.htm.

OECD. (2022d). *TOSSD reporting instructions.* www.tossd.org/docs/reporting- instructions.pdf.

Oxfam. (2014). *A dangerous diversion: Will the IFC's flagship health PPP bankrupt Lesotho's ministry of health?* https://oxfamilibrary.openrepository .com/bitstream/handle/10546/315183/bn-dangerous-diversion-lesotho- health-ppp-070414-en.pdf?sequence=1.

Oxford Business Group. (n.d.). *A change of tack: Greater cooperation between public and private could bring rewards.* 2 November 2021, https://oxfordbu sinessgroup.com/analysis/change-tack-greater-cooperation-between-public- and-private-could-bring-rewards.

Parlimen Malaysia. (2005). *Penyata Rasmi Parlimen Dewan Rakyat: Selasa 29 November 2005.*

Pearson, N. (2022, April 5). *Why Kenyan nonprofit Jacaranda health spun out its hospital as a social venture.* ImpactAlpha. https://impactalpha.com/why- kenyan-nonprofit-jacaranda-health-spun-out-its-hospital-as-a-social-ven ture/.

Pfeiffer, J. (2013). The struggle for a public sector: PEPFAR in Mozambique. In Biehl J., & Petryna, A. (Eds.), *When People Come First: Critical Studies in Global Health: Critical Studies in Global Health* (pp. 166–81). Princeton University Press.

PharmAccess Group. (2021). *Stichting medical credit fund: Annual report 2020.*

Philips. (2010). *Annual report 2009. Staying focused, acting decisively.*

Philips. (2013a). *Annual report 2012. Accelerate! progress in delivering our full potential.*

Philips. (2013b). *Fabric of Africa trends report.*

Philips. (2015a). *Annual report 2014. Innovating for a healthier, more sustain- able world.*

Philips. (2015b). *Working together to transform: Healthcare in Africa.* www .philips.com/c-dam/corporate/about-philips/sustainability/healthy-people/fab ric-of-africa/focus/Philips_Working_together_to_transform_HC_in_Africa.pdf

Philips. (2016, June 12). *Philips community life center.* www.philips.co.ke/a-w/ about/news/archive/healthcare/news/press/2016/2016-06-12_Philips- Community-Life-Center.html.

Philips. (2021, March 8). *Philips and the Dutch development bank FMO combine forces to accelerate universal health coverage in Africa*. www .philips.com/a-w/about/news/archive/standard/news/articles/2021/ 20210308-philips-and-the-dutch-development-bank-fmo-combine-forces-to-accelerate-universal-health-coverage-in-africa.html.

Pilla, V. (2022, February 24). *Vasan Eye Care creditors approve ASG's 600-cr bid*. The Economic Times. https://economictimes.indiatimes.com/industry/ healthcare/biotech/vasan-eye-care-creditors-approve-asgs-600-cr-bid/article show/89783558.cms.

Proparco. (2006). *Rapport annuel 2005*.

Proparco. (2009). *Annual report 08*.

Proparco. (2011, October 31). *Loan to Hospital Do Coracao to improve and develop the healthcare services of a reputed Brazilian hospital*. www.pro parco.fr/en/carte-des-projets/hcor.

Proparco. (2013). *Annual report 2012*.

Proparco. (2014a). *Annual report 2013*.

Proparco. (2014b, December 19). *Six hospitals to scale up healthcare provision: The Adana hospital complex*. www.proparco.fr/en/carte-des-projets/adana-hospital.

Proparco. (2014c, December 31). *Towards a regional healthcare facility network in the Maghreb region: The ambitious objective of NAHHG*. www .proparco.fr/en/carte-des-projets/nahhg.

Proparco. (2015a). *Annual report 2014*.

Proparco. (2015b). *In Sub-Saharan Africa, the private sector is addressing the lack of healthcare provision*. www.proparco.fr/en/carte-des-projets/ciel-healthcare-ltd.

Proparco. (2015c, May 29). *Supporting the development of the hospital and pharmaceutical sectors in South and Southeast Asia*. www.proparco.fr/en/ carte-des-projets/quadria-fund-2015.

Proparco. (2016a, September 6). *Evex: A loan to upgrade hospital services in Georgia*. www.proparco.fr/en/carte-des-projets/evex-medical.

Proparco. (2016b, December 14). *A new financial instrument for Proparco's social projects: Green & Social Project Bonds to fund a new hospital in Turkey*. www.proparco.fr/en/actualites/new-financial-instrument-proparcos-social-projects-green-social-project-bonds-fund-new.

Proparco. (2017, April 14). *Turkey: €15 million to support a PPP public hospital-building project*. www.proparco.fr/en/actualites/turkey-eu15-million-support-ppp-public-hospital-building-project.

Proparco. (2018). *Developing health services in East Africa with AAR health-care*. www.proparco.fr/en/carte-des-projets/aar-healthcare.

Proparco. (2019, October 22). *MetaMed*. www.proparco.fr/en/carte-des-pro jets/metamed.

Proparco. (2020, June 30). *IFC, IFU and PROPARCO are making an equity investment of over USD 100m to improve the health sector in Egypt and Morocco*. www.proparco.fr/en/carte-des-projets/humania.

Pulse. (2017, November 3). Korea's KDB infra to invest $63 mn in Turkish general hospital. https://pulsenews.co.kr/view.php?year=2017&no= 729021.

Quadir, F. (2013). Rising donors and the new narrative of 'South–South' cooperation: What prospects for changing the landscape of development assistance programmes? *Third World Quarterly, 34*(2), 321–38. https://doi .org/10.1080/01436597.2013.775/88.

Quadria Capital. (2021). *Portfolio*. www.quadriacapital.com/portfolio/invest ments/.

Rai, J. (2018, July 4). *Asian Development Bank to invest in dialysis firm DCDC*. VCCircle. www.vccircle.com/asian-development-bank-to-invest-in-dialy sis-firm-dcdc.

Rajagopal, D. (2017, April 13). *Dr Mohan's raises Rs 66 crore from Lok capital, Evolvence*. The Economic Times. https://economictimes.indiatimes.com/ industry/healthcare/biotech/dr-mohans-raises-rs-66-crore-from-lok-capital- evolvence/articleshow/58161679.cms.

Rao, M. (1999). *Disinvesting in Health: The World Bank's Prescriptions for Health*. SAGE.

Rediff.com. (2004, August 10). *Temasek set to buy 5% Apollo Hospitals stake*. www.rediff.com/money/report/apollo/20040810.htm.Renault, P., & Rousselot, M. (2013, July). Meeting the financing needs of healthcare providers. *Private Sector & Development*. https://issuu.com/objectif-developpement/docs/ proparco_revuespd_17_uk.

Reuters. (2001, April 27). *Mahathir's son quits corporate roles*. CNN.Com. http://edition.cnn.com/2001/BUSINESS/asia/04/27/malaysia.mahathir.biz/ index.html.

Reuters. (2012, February 21). *Abraaj acquires Aureos capital to strengthen emerging market PE biz*. www.reuters.com/article/abraaj-acquires-aureos- capital-to-streng-idINDEE81K05620120221.

Reuters. (2013, March 12). *Temasek bets $25.7 million in healthCare global; EILSF exits with 2.2x returns*. www.reuters.com/article/temasek-bets-257- million-in-healthcare-g-idINDEE92B04J20130312.

Reuters. (2020, December 28). *UPDATE 1-Vietnam's Vingroup sells stake in medical unit to Singapore's GIC*. www.reuters.com/article/gic-vingroup- vinmec-idUSL1N2J80C5.

Riddell, R. C. (1999). The end of foreign aid to Africa? Concerns about donor policies. *African Affairs*, *98*(392), 309–35. https://doi.org/10.1093/oxford journals.afraf.a008042.

Rijksdienst voor Ondernemend Nederland. (2017, March 1). *Scoping study TA project 'PPP in LS&H sector Kenya'*. https://projects.rvo.nl/project/nl-kvk-27378529-mag17ke02/.

RMBV. (2021). *Fund platforms*. www.rmbv.net/platforms.

Roberts, S. M. (2014). Development capital: USAID and the rise of development contractors. *Annals of the Association of American Geographers*, *104* (5), 1030–51. https://doi.org/10.1080/00045608.2014.924749.

Rushton, S. (2011). Global health security: Security for whom? Security from what? *Political Ṣtudies*, *59*(4), 779–96. https://doi.org/10.1111/j.1467-9248.2011.00919.x.

Rushton, S., & Williams, O. D. (2011). *Partnerships and Foundations in Global Health Governance*. Palgrave Macmillan.

Sakra World Hospital. (2022). *International patient services*. www.sakraworld hospital.com/international-service.

Salm, M., Ali, M., Minihane, M., & Conrad, P. (2021). Defining global health: Findings from a systematic review and thematic analysis of the literature. *BMJ Global Health*, *6*(6), e005292. https://doi.org/10.1136/bmjgh-2021-005292.

Samsung C&T. (2019, July 26). *Efforts to improve Mongolian medical services bear fruit after three years*. http://news.samsungcnt.com/efforts-improve-mongolian-medical-services-bear-fruit-three-years/.

Samsung C&T. (2022). *Infrastructure | overview*. http://project.samsungcnt .com/spb/infra/0401/html.do.

Santelli, J. S., Kantor, L. M., Grilo, S. A. et al. (2017). Abstinence-only-until-marriage: An updated review of U.S. policies and programs and their impact. *Journal of Adolescent Health*, *61*(3), 273–80. https://doi.org/10.1016/ j.jadohealth.2017.05.031.

Sapkala, Y. (2010, June 4). *Fortis' Parkway battle: The Khazanah story*. Moneylife. www.moneylife.in/article/fortis-parkway-battle-the-khazanah-story/5843.html.

Satya Capital. (2009). *Hygeia secures financial partnerships to support growth plans*. www.satyacapital.com/news/hygeia-secures-financial-partnerships .html.

Savoy, C. M., Carter, P., & Lemma, A. (2016). *Development finance institutions come of age: Policy engagement, impact and new directions*. https:// edfi-website-v1.s3.fr-par.scw.cloud/uploads/2017/10/Development-Finance-Institutions-Come-of-Age.pdf.

Scandinavian Care. (2021). *Investment and consulting.* www.scandinaviancare
.com/investment-and-consulting.

Schmidt, H. (2003). Pushed to the front: The foreign assistance policy of the
Federal Republic of Germany, 1958–1971. *Contemporary European History,
12*(4), 473–507. https://doi.org/10.1017/S0960777303001383.

Schrecker, T. (2020). Towards a critical political economy of global health. In
C. McInnes, K. Lee, & J. Youde (Eds.), *The Oxford Handbook of Global
Health Politics* (pp. 468–90). Oxford University Press. https://doi.org/
10.1093/oxfordhb/9780190456818.013.29.

Selbervik, H., & Nygaard, K. (2006). *Nordic exceptionalism in development
assistance? Aid policies and the major donors: The Nordic countries.* www
.cmi.no/publications/file/2371-nordic-exceptionalism-in-development-assist
ance.pdf.

Sell, S. K., & Williams, O. D. (2020). Health under capitalism: A global political
economy of structural pathogenesis. *Review of International Political
Economy, 27*(1), 1–25. https://doi.org/10.1080/09692290.2019.1659842.

Sheares. (2022). *About us | overview.* www.sheareshealthcare.com/about-us/
overview/.

Shin, J., & Chang, H. (2003). *Restructuring 'Korea Inc.': Financial Crisis,
Corporate Reform, and Institutional Transition.* RoutledgeCurzon.

Shukla, T. (2016, January 29). *What really happened at Vasan healthcare?*
Mint. www.livemint.com/Companies/0XHIPMIRMI5BeUMeZQEhoN/
What-really-happened-at-Vasan-Healthcare.html.

Silva, A. L., Bernardo, L. B., & Mah, L. (2021). *The future of international
development cooperation: Fragmentation, adaptation and innovation in
a changing world.* www.plataformaongd.pt/uploads/subcanais2/the_future_
of_international_development_cooperation_english_final.pdf.

Singh, K. (2008, August 16). *PEs eye standalone regional hospitals.* Economic
Times. https://economictimes.indiatimes.com/industry/banking/finance/pes-
eye-standalone-regional-hospitals/articleshow/3369420.cms.

Singh, K. (2010, December 24). *Temasek buys 3% pie in Max India.* The
Economic Times. https://economictimes.indiatimes.com/industry/health
care/biotech/healthcare/temasek-buys-3-pie-in-max-india/articleshow/
7154213.cms?from=mdr.

Singh, K., & Chatterjee, P. (2011, June 22). *Vasan healthcare may sell 15% to
GIC for $100 million.* The Economic Times. https://economictimes.india
times.com/industry/healthcare/biotech/healthcare/vasan-healthcare-may-
sell-15-to-gic-for-100-million/articleshow/8945310.cms?from=mdr.

Sirio-Libanes Hospital. (2014). *Sustainability report 2014.* https://media.gra
phassets.com/ZriWlcQrudxVCmBn4QQ4.

Skelcher, C. (2000). Changing images of the State: Overloaded, hollowed-out, congested. *Public Policy and Administration*, *15*(3), 3–19. https://doi.org/10.1177/095207670001500302.

Skocpol, T. (1985). Bringing the state back in: Strategies of analysis in current research. In P. B. Evans, D. Rueschemeyer, & T. Skocpol (Eds.), *Bringing the State Back In* (pp. 3–38). Cambridge University Press.

Sojitz. (2017, July 21). *Sojitz joins hospital project in the Republic of Turkey.* www.sojitz.com/en/news/2017/07/20170721-02.php.

Sojitz. (2020a). *Sojitz opens one of the world's largest hospital complexes in Turkey.* www.sojitz.com/en/news/2020/05/20200521.php.

Sojitz. (2020b, September). *Medical infrastructure business.* www.sojitz.com/en/special/projects/detail/post-6.php.

Sonavane, R. (2021, September 30). *Carlyle to part-exit as Medanta hospital chain files for IPO.* VCCircle. www.vccircle.com/carlyle-to-part-exit-as-medanta-hospital-chain-files-for-ipo.

Sonmez, M. (2021, June 30). *Turkish-Danish hospital deal might be more than meets the eye.* Al-Monitor. www.al-monitor.com/originals/2021/06/turkish-danish-hospital-deal-might-be-more-meets-eye.

Sovereign Wealth Fund Institute. (2022). *Top 100 largest sovereign wealth fund rankings by total assets.* www.swfinstitute.org/fund-rankings/sovereign-wealth-fund.

Sperber, N. (2019). The many lives of state capitalism: From classical Marxism to free-market advocacy. *History of the Human Sciences*, *32*(3), 100–24. https://doi.org/10.1177/0952695118815553.

Sridhar, D., Winters, J., & Strong, E. (2017). World Bank's financing, priorities, and lending structures for global health. *BMJ*, *38*, j3339.

Stein, F. (2021). Risky business: COVAX and the financialization of global vaccine equity. *Globalization and Health*, *17*(1), 112. https://doi.org/10.1186/s12992-021-00763-8.

Stein, F., & Sridhar, D. (2018). The financialisation of global health. *Wellcome Open Research*, *3*, 17. https://doi.org/10.12688/wellcomeopenres.13885.1.

Stenberg, K., Hanssen, O., Edejer, T. T.-T. et al. (2017). Financing transformative health systems towards achievement of the health Sustainable Development Goals: A model for projected resource needs in 67 low-income and middle-income countries. *The Lancet Global Health*, *5*(9), e875–e887. https://doi.org/10.1016/S2214-109X(17)30263-2.

Storm, S. (2018). Financialization and economic development: A debate on the social efficiency of modern finance. *Development and Change*, *49*(2), 302–29. https://doi.org/10.1111/dech.12385.

Swedfund. (2010a). *Finance for development: Swedfund sustainability report 2009.*

Swedfund. (2010b). *Swedfund annual report 2009.*

Swedfund. (2012). *Elekta and Swedfund invest in radiosurgery and radiotherapy clinics.*

Swedfund. (2013a). *Poverty reduction through sustainable business: Swedfund's sustainability and annual report 2012.*

Swedfund. (2013b). *Poverty reduction through sustainable business: Swedfund's sustainability And annual report 2012.*

Swedfund. (2014). *Growing power: How Swedfund helps fight poverty through sustainable business [Integrated report 2013].*

Swedfund. (2020a). *Sustainable Investments: A true story about escaping poverty [Integrated report 2019].*

Swedfund. (2020b, April 2). *Swedfund invests in maternal care in East Africa.* https://www.swedfund.se/en/about-swedfund/mynewsdesk/#/pressreleases/swedfund-invests-in-maternal-care-in-east-africa-2988127

Swedfund. (2022). *Investments.* www.swedfund.se/en/investments/.

Tan, Y., Lee, K., & Pang, T. (2012). Global health governance and the rise of Asia. *Global Policy, 3*(3), 324–35. https://doi.org/10.1111/j.1758-5899.2012.00177.x.

Task Force Health Care. (2017, May 3). *Philips partners with the government of Kenya and the UN to advance the African healthcare agenda.* www.tfhc.nl/philips-partners-government-kenya-un-advance-african-healthcare-agenda/.

Task Force Health Care, & Kenya Healthcare Federation. (2016). *Kenyan healthcare sector: opportunities for the Dutch life sciences & health sector.* https://khf.co.ke/wp-content/uploads/2021/01/2016-Kenyan-Healthcare-Sector-Report.pdf.

Temasek. (2005). *Reshaping our portfolio: Temasek review 2005.* www.temasek.com.sg/content/dam/temasek-corporate/our-financials/investor-library/annual-review/en-tr-thumbnail-and-pdf/temasek-review-2005.pdf.

Temasek. (2006). *Istithmar and Temasek invest in Bumrungrad.* www.temasek.com.sg/en/news-and-views/news-room/news/2006/istithmar-and-temasek-invest-in-bumrungrad.

The Economic Times. (2010, July 4). *Axis, IDBI Bank led consortium to fund Fortis' Parkway buy.* https://economictimes.indiatimes.com/industry/healthcare/biotech/healthcare/axis-idbi-bank-led-consortium-to-fund-fortis-parkway-buy/articleshow/6127137.cms?from=mdr

The Economic Times. (2021, September 16). Ayu Health Gets $6.3-million Funding from Vertex, Stellaris and Others. *The Economic Times.* https://economictimes.indiatimes.com/tech/funding/ayu-health-gets-6-3-million-funding-from-vertex-stellaris-and-others/articleshow/86261195.cms.

The G20 Research Group. (2015). *G20. Turkey: The Antalya Summit*. www .g7g20.com/publication/g20-2015

The Korea Times. (2012). *Samsung C&T picked as prime bidder for hospital project in Turkey*. www.koreatimes.co.kr/www/tech/2021/09/129_125174.html

The Star. (2006, January 21). Temasek and UAE firm buy 12% of Thai hospital. www.thestar.com.my/business/business-news/2006/01/21/temasek-and-uae-firm-buy-12-of-thai-hospital/.

The Star. (2021, May 7). *Mitsui & Co weighs buyout of US$11bil hospital group IHH Healthcare*. www.thestar.com.my/business/business-news/2021/05/07/mitsui–co-weighs-buyout-of-us11bil-hospital-group-ihh-healthcare

Toyota Tsusho. (2016, July 1). *Raising the quality of medical care in India through hospital management*. www.toyota-tsusho.com/english/about/pro ject/02.html.

UK Government. (2017). *Capital increase to CDC, the UK's development finance institution*. https://assets.publishing.service.gov.uk/government/uploads/sys tem/uploads/attachment_data/file/651848/2017_to_2021_CDC_capital_increase_business_case_publication_1038.pdf.

UK Government. (2021, November 24). *Truss revamps British development finance institution to deliver jobs and clean growth*. www.gov.uk/govern ment/news/truss-revamps-british-development-finance-institution-to-deliver-jobs-and-clean-growth.

UNCTAD. (2014, October 21). *Developing countries and sovereign wealth funds ready for partnership on sustainable investment*. https://unctad.org/press-material/developing-countries-and-sovereign-wealth-funds-ready-part nership-sustainable.

UNDP. (2021, December 19). *Kenya SDG partnership platform*. Trust Fund Factsheet. https://mptf.undp.org/factsheet/fund/KEN00?fund_status_month_to=&fund_status_year_to=2017.

United Nations. (2015). *The Addis Ababa action agenda of the third inter-national conference on financing for development*. https://sustainabledevelop ment.un.org/content/documents/2051AAAA_Outcome.pdf.

van Dam, P., & van Dis, W. (2014). Beyond the merchant and the clergyman: Assessing moral claims about development cooperation. *Third World Quarterly, 35*(9), 1636–55. https://doi.org/10.1080/01436597.2014.970863.

van de Pas, R., & van Schaik, L. G. (2014). Democratizing the World Health Organization. *Public Health, 128*(2), 195–201. https://doi.org/10.1016/j.puhe .2013.08.023.

VCCircle. (2010, December 16). Aureos capital India invests $10m in BSR super speciality hospitals. www.reuters.com/article/idINIndia-53614620 101216.

Venkat, P. R., Holmes, S., & Tudor, A. (2010, July 27). An uncommon deal battle ends. *Wall Street Journal*. www.wsj.com/articles/SB10001424052748 703700904575390491799022242.

Verger, A. (2012). Framing and selling global education policy: The promotion of public–private partnerships for education in low-income contexts. *Journal of Education Policy*, *27*(1), 109–30. https://doi.org/10.1080/02680939 .2011.623242.

Wade, R. H. (2018). The developmental state: Dead or alive? *Development and Change*, *49*(2), 518–46. https://doi.org/10.1111/dech.12381.

Wadge, H., Roy, R., Sripathy, A. et al. (2017a). How to harness the private sector for universal health coverage. *The Lancet*, *390*(10090), e19–e20. https://doi.org/10.1016/S0140-6736(17)31718-X.

Wadge, H., Roy, R., Sripathy, A. et al. (2017b). *Evaluating the Impact of Private Providers on Health and Health Systems*. London.

Wang, X., & Sun, T. (2014). China's engagement in global health governance: A critical analysis of China's assistance to the health sector of Africa. *Journal of Global Health*, *4*(1), 010301. https://doi.org/10.7189/jogh.04.010301.

Wemos. (2019). *Best public value for public money: The case of match-funded multi-hospital infrastructure development in Tanzania*. www.wemos.nl/wp-content/uploads/2019/11/Wemos_discussion-paper_Aid-for-Trade_Best-Public-Value-for-Public-Money_Oct-2019.pdf.

Wemos. (2020). *In the interest of health for all? The Dutch 'aid and trade' agenda as pursued in the African healthcare context*. www.wemos.nl/wp-content/uploads/2020/10/Dutch-AT-in-Health-Kenya_Wemos-discussion-paper_Oct-2020.pdf.

White, G., & Wade, R. (1984). Developmental states in East Asia: Editorial introduction. *IDS Bulletin*, *15*(2), 1–3. https://doi.org/10.1111/j.1759-5436.1984.mp15002001.x.

Wong, J. (2004). The adaptive developmental state in East Asia. *Journal of East Asian Studies*, *4*(3), 345–62. https://doi.org/10.1017/S1598240800006007.

Woo-Cumings, M. (1999). *The Developmental State*. Cornell University Press.

World Bank. (2013a). *Financing for development post-2015*.

World Bank. (2013b). *Public private partnerships for health: PPPs are here and growing*.

World Bank, & International Monetary Fund. (2015). *From billions to trillions: Transforming development finance*.

Wright, M., Wood, G., Musacchio, A. et al. (2021). State capitalism in international context: Varieties and variations. *Journal of World Business*, *56*(2), 101160. https://doi.org/10.1016/j.jwb.2020.101160.

Wynne, M. (2000, April). *Health services in Singapore*. Corporate Healthcare. www.bmartin.cc/dissent/documents/health/singapore.html.

Wynne, M. (2004). *The companies buying Mayne health 2003*. https://docu ments.uow.edu.au/~bmartin/dissent/documents/health/mayne_purchasers .html.

Yasutomo, D. T. (1989). Why aid? Japan as an 'aid great power'. *Pacific Affairs*, *62*(4), 490–503. https://doi.org/10.2307/2759672.

Yilmaz, V. (2017). *The Politics of Healthcare Reform in Turkey*. Palgrave Macmillan.

You, J. (2021). The changing dynamics of state–business relations and the politics of reform and capture in South Korea. *Review of International Political Economy*, *28*(1), 81–102. https://doi.org/10.1080/09692290.2020 .1724176.

Youde, J. (2012). *Global Health Governance*. Polity Press.

Youde, J. (2013). The Rockefeller and Gates Foundations in global health governance. *Global Society*, *27*(2), 139–58. https://doi.org/10.1080/ 13600826.2012.762341.

Youde, J. (2018a). China's role in global health governance. In R. Parker & J. Garcia (Eds.), *Routledge Handbook on the Politics of Global Health* (pp. 172–80). Routledge.

Youde, J. (2018b). *China, International Society, and Global Health Governance* (Vol. 1). Oxford University Press. https://doi.org/10.1093/oso/ 9780198813057.003.0008.

Zhao, Y., Micah, A. E., Gloyd, S., & Dieleman, J. L. (2020). Development assistance for health and the Middle East and North Africa. *Globalization and Health*, *16*(1), 14. https://doi.org/10.1186/s12992-020-0545-z.

Cambridge Elements ≡

Global Development Studies

Peter Ho
Zhejiang University

Peter Ho is Distinguished Professor at Zhejiang University and high-level National Expert of China. He has held or holds the position of, amongst others, Research Professor at the London School of Economics and Political Science and the School of Oriental and African Studies, Full Professor at Leiden University and Director of the Modern East Asia Research Centre, Full Professor at Groningen University and Director of the Centre for Development Studies. Ho is well-cited and published in leading journals of development, planning and area studies. He published numerous books, including with *Cambridge University Press, Oxford University Press*, and *Wiley-Blackwell*. Ho achieved the William Kapp Prize, China Rural Development Award, and European Research Council Consolidator Grant He chairs the International Conference on Agriculture and Rural Development (www.icardc .org) and sits on the boards of Land Use Policy, Conservation and Society, China Rural Economics, Journal of Peasant Studies, and other journals.

Servaas Storm
Delft University of Technology

Servaas Storm is a Dutch economist who has published widely on issues of macroeconomics, development, income distribution & economic growth, finance, and climate change. He is a Senior Lecturer at Delft University of Technology. He obtained a PhD in Economics (in 1992) from Erasmus University Rotterdam and worked as consultant for the ILO and UNCTAD. His latest book, co-authored with C.W.M. Naastepad, is *Macroeconomics Beyond the NAIRU* (Harvard University Press, 2012) and was awarded with the 2013 Myrdal Prize of the European Association for Evolutionary Political Economy. Servaas Storm is one of the editors of *Development and Change* (2006-now) and a member of the Institute for New Economic Thinking's Working Group on the Political Economy of Distribution.

Advisory Board

Arun Agrawal, *University of Michigan*
Jun Borras, *International Institute of Social Studies*
Daniel Bromley, *University of Wisconsin-Madison*
Jane Carruthers, *University of South Africa*
You-tien Hsing, *University of California, Berkeley*
Tamara Jacka, *Australian National University*

About the Series

The Cambridge Elements on Global Development Studies publishes ground-breaking, novel works that move beyond existing theories and methodologies of development in order to consider social change in real times and real spaces.

Cambridge Elements ☰

Global Development Studies

Elements in the Series

Printed in the United States
by Baker & Taylor Publisher Services